GROOMED

Jerome L. Whitehead

PAGE PUBLISHING, INC.
New York, NY

First originally published by Page Publishing, Inc. 2017

ISBN978-1-64082-564-2 (Paperback)
ISBN 978-1-64082-565-9 (Digital)

Printed in the United States of America

CONTENTS

INTRODUCTION

As far back as I can remember, I've always thought that something was wrong with me. For all intents and purposes, normality eluded me. Sometimes, it would be just within my grasp. Sometimes, it would be this tangible thing that I could almost touch and feel, and for a moment, all would be right with the world. Then, it would slip through my fingers, and I would find myself falling again.

Falling was my norm. Not having a steady surface to plant my feet down on became my way of life. Treading water emotionally was what I had become used to, and this process continued for years, but because it was normal to tread water, it never occurred to me to wonder why this battle was so hard. Why was living from day to day such a challenge for me?

I thought that maybe the way that I was, was the way God intended me to be. I never thought that there was something much larger than myself going on ... things that I never took into consideration. I didn't know suffering wore many masks, and that I had gotten so used to wearing mine, I couldn't distinguish between what was normal and what wasn't. The only thing I knew was what was.

I turned fifty-one today. It was today that I decided to write this book. Only now are the clouds starting to disperse, and I'm getting a peek at the rays of sunshine that come after a storm. Realization and self-awareness are a funny thing. Some people say that it is all about perspective. I have a tendency to agree. Perspective, after all, is 99 percent reality. I've gained some insight into who I am, who I would have been under different circumstances, and who I strive to be. I used to dismiss certain behaviors I exhibited as defects of character, shortcomings that I simply would have to learn to live with. I allowed myself to be manipulated into situations I used to wish I could take back and do over. I realize now it's those situations as well as the good ones that have helped shape me into the man that I ultimately became. And because of that, I don't want a do-over as much as I would like to build on what I have going for me right now. Being African American and being gay have had its high and low points. I haven't always been proud to belong to the LGBTQ community, but I realize that loving yourself includes embracing who you are now, the good and the bad, as well as who you want to be.

As a journalist, I've had the privilege of speaking with men and women that are survivors of childhood sexual abuse. I've read their stories, talked with them at length, and written articles about them. But this past year, I met an author whose work gave me my aha moment. Author Carter Lee wrote a book entitled *When Jonathan Cried for Me*. What I initially thought was going to be a routine interview and book review turned out to be so much more. It gave me the courage to tell my story. Most men who are childhood sexual abuse survivors don't willingly talk about their experiences. The fact that Carter was a man stood out for me since I had read many stories dealing with this topic. Most books that are released dealing with issues of sexual abuse are written by female survivors. Very rarely did I ever hear the stories told from a male perspective.

Gay men don't really talk about being abuse survivors because I think that those of us that have gone through this type of trauma don't really believe that any psychological damage had been done. Gay men love being intimate with men. It's natural for us. For heterosexual men, being sexually intimate with another man isn't normal, and therefore, it may cause feelings of anger and rage to play itself out in their lives until they are forced to seek some type of help before their lives spiral completely out of control. For some heterosexual men, the emotion thrown out of whack for them may very well be anger. For the author Carter Lee, his anger would touch down like a twister out of the blue and leave just as quickly. It made me wonder that if anger was the emotion that was thrown out of whack for him, what was the emotion that was thrown out of whack for me?

To answer this question, I had to think back over my life and reflect on situations that I had carefully packed away in emotional boxes and put on shelves to never be rethought about again. As I unpacked these boxes and pulled out these memories, I can now see what was out of place for me. And we all know that when you are aware of a problem and can see it under your mind's eye, you can fix it.

All my life, I felt this overwhelming need to be accepted. I needed to be included, and with that inclusion came the validation of who I was at the time, as well as who I wanted to be. It was that simple, and yet it explained so much.

Groomed was written not just for gay men but also for any man that has had their emotions compromised by someone that may have taken their innocence away from them. I'm here to tell you that you can build on what was lost. Even if you can't reclaim the years you've spent being who you are, you don't have to remain there. You can rebuild, perhaps even reclaim who you would have been. It is also written for single women who have children, although a married woman may gain some insight from this work as well. This book gives an up close and personal insight into the mind of an abuse victim. It may also provide you with some of the questions that you may ask yourself and your child should you suspect that they may be the victim of a sexual predator.

Being a strong, opinionated, confident black man is what I always wanted to be. What I've found is that I am so much more. I've lived in this dark area for forty-five years. Now I'm ready to walk into the warmth of the sunshine and claim what was inside of me all along. Forty-five years of being in the dark is long enough.

I'm ready to walk into the light. I hope that you can come with me.

SUNNY DAYS

I was a "daddy's boy" for as long as I can remember. Some boys are "momma's boys," and I'm sure that we've all heard that terminology and know all too well what it means. Me, I was a "daddy's boy." I looked just like my father. I was the firstborn of four boys, and when my mother gave birth to me, I can say that I was the spitting image of him. I loved my father like no other. I say this because for as long as I can remember, my father was the epitome of strength and courage. Well, he was until some of the choices he made adversely impacted our family. I loved him very much then, and I love him now; it's just that it's taken me years to learn *how* to love him without getting my feelings hurt. My father was a strong, somewhat loud man, but his laugh was infectious, and I remember wanting to do anything to make him happy.

I guess part of me knew of his darker side. He had a temper and a strong hand. He came from the old school where men ruled their families...sometimes in lieu of loving them. He had this uncanny ability to silence you with a look. Instinctively, I knew when to be quiet and when it was okay to speak. He was handsome, rugged, and he loved music. I know that I get my love of music from him. He had a hi-fi system that seemed like it took up the entire length of the wall in our living room. There were two stacks of forty-fives and a multitude of albums inside, and I could read the labels to each of the records with perfect comprehension at an early age. This was something that made him proud, and I was so glad that I could do something that made him proud of me. It was almost as if we shared a secret that his friends didn't know about until he told them to pick out any 45 in the record player and give it to me to read. His friends thought he coached me. He told them with pride that he didn't. He simply said that "his boy is smart!" With all of that, I knew how to behave around him. I knew when to be quiet because if I didn't, out would come the belt, and he could wield it better than any slave master. One or two whippings convinced me to keep in line and stay in line for as long as he was around. Still, I idolized him because even with his temper, I knew that he loved me and my mother.

My mother was beautiful. I know that every boy says this about their mother, but this was definitely the case with mine. She used to wear full-cap wigs, and she loved to take pictures. I understood why. She had beautiful eyes, huge almond-shaped eyes that were as insightful as they were deep brown. When my parents were together, I knew that my mother had a temper, but out of the two, I feared my father more. My mother was a true nurturer, but I believe this was because my father was the disciplinarian. She came from the old school as well, and I believe that she thought that a woman's place was to submit to her husband … at least to a certain extent. She was an excellent homemaker, and when it came to her children, she didn't play. She would put me and my brothers before him in a heartbeat, which oftentimes didn't go over well with my dad. Still, back when my parents were together, she didn't have to play the roles of both the nurturer and disciplinarian, at least not at that time anyway. It wouldn't be until much later that I would find out that the temper of a single female parent is much worse than a father of a family any day of the week.

I'm a '60s baby, born in Newark, New Jersey. My life started with me being around my father's family, which entailed us visiting my grandparents frequently. I can still remember getting into my father's tan Pontiac LeMans and making the drive over to see them. We went on Sundays, and one of the things that I used to love doing was sitting at my grandfather's feet while watching the *Wonderful World of Disney*. I couldn't have cared less what was going on around me. For that moment, it was just me and my grandfather. In many ways, he was my safe spot even though I didn't realize it at the time. He was the man that offset the perceived coldness of my grandmother. Thinking back, I realize that my father looked almost exactly like him. The resemblance was astounding.

My grandparents lived on a street that was located literally about half a block away from a busy highway. I can remember hearing the trucks roll by as we ascended the few steps to the porch to see Grandmommy and Granddaddy. Ida Whitehead was a tough old woman who had love in her heart, but you had to get past the tough exterior to see it. My grandfather, James Whitehead, was kind, always smiling, which would explain why I gravitated toward him. At that time, my father's youngest brother and sister still lived at home. They lived in a two-bedroom apartment that ran the length of the entire first floor of the building that they resided in. Once you walked down a short corridor to enter their living space, you had to make a sharp turn to the right, and you would find yourself in a small living room. I believe that it was my grandmother that kept the huge rotating candy dish full of caramels with the white creamy center, mint balls, Mary Janes, and various hard candies. Oddly enough, I don't remember any paintings on the walls.

Memories are funny and very selective. I believe the human mind remembers the highs and lows, much like black and white. It's the in between or gray areas that get a little convoluted. I can remember things like my grandmother's lazy Susan filled with candy that sat on the coffee table. I can remember the huge room that served as my uncle's bedroom with a huge leather-backed chair that sat in the corner directly in front of the floor-model color television set that Granddaddy liked to watch so often. I remember the kitchen with its mint-colored walls that sat just beyond the room that served as my uncle's bedroom, and it was in that kitchen that I remember the loving smells the most: the aroma of frying chicken, catfish cornbread, and black-eyed peas wafting through the room were not uncommon. But I don't remember any artwork that my grandmother may have had, only black-and-white pictures of family members. I couldn't tell you what color the living room sofa was. That's what I mean by the in between or gray areas. I know that there was a bathroom, and I know that my grandparents had their own bedroom, and I know that I may have gone into those rooms before; I just don't remember them.

Motown was popping back then, and I didn't know of any black family that didn't have a couple of 45s by the Supremes, the Temptations, Stevie Wonder, or Smokey. When my father was in a good mood, I could remember hearing the tunes of James Brown, Chuck Jackson, and Ike and Tina Turner blasting from the hi-fi.

It seemed like life was simpler then. The milkman brought quarts of milk and left them in a metal container outside of our door in the back. My mother would fix huge plates of food for my father. What stands out for me was corned beef and cabbage. I don't know if this was his favorite, or if I just happened to notice that his plate was overflowing with food whenever she prepared it for him. I just remember thinking, "How is he going to eat all of this?" But he could ... very easily. He could eat that and drink a quart of milk in one sitting.

I remember us living relatively well. We had a floor model color television set, the hi-fi, a family car, and I don't ever remember going to bed hungry. One of my father's favorite pastimes was playing cards. For a brief period, all was right with the world even with its imperfections and idiosyncrasies. I had learned not to cry in front of my father because that wasn't the thing a boy was supposed to do. As long as I adhered to the rules that he set forth, everything was good, and for most of the time, things were. It wasn't until a few years later when the storm clouds began to gather, and my world would suddenly start to change.

THAT FIRST TOUCH

I was six years of age when my younger brother was born. I don't remember the conversation or explanation (if any) to tell me where he came from. But I do remember being happy when he arrived. It was also around this time that life began to change for me. My father would periodically drop me off at my grandparents' house for them to watch me if he had to work. I believe that this is why I wound up staying there overnight this particular evening. I told you that my youngest aunt and uncle still lived at home. They were both in their teens. My being a boy meant that I had to share a bed with my uncle, which was fine with me.

I didn't like being away from my parents or sleeping in a bed that wasn't mine, but I was still with my family, and I dealt with it as best as I could.

At three o'clock in the morning, my uncle awakened me. I remember the time because a clock/radio sat on the headboard of his bed. The clock's face illuminated a dull orange color that I remember staring at intently at the time. My uncle was a teenager, strong, handsome in his own way, with a fair complexion. I wasn't alarmed or afraid when he awakened me nor was I anxious. I just remember thinking that the whole house was completely dark, and I was acutely aware that there was no one around but me and him. He asked me if I loved him, and I remember telling him yes. He said "good." Without saying another word, he pulled me on top of him and kissed me on the mouth. His breath smelled like him, neither bad nor good, but as he gyrated underneath me, I remember getting an erection... at least as much as a six-year-old could get an erection while hearing the trucks roll by on the highway less than a block away.

I wish I could tell you that this was a horrible experience. I wish I could tell you that it felt as awful as you as a reader may probably think this is, but the truth of the matter is, it wasn't. When African American actor and filmmaker Tyler Perry talked about his experience with molestation, he said that his body betrayed him. Honestly, I think that's what happens to most boys when confronted with this type of activity. If it's not overtly painful, then your body is going to respond. My uncle didn't penetrate me. He didn't force me to suck his dick. He simply pulled me on top of him in the middle of the night and gyrated underneath me until he came.

But simply because he didn't painfully violate me physically doesn't mean that I wasn't violated. He violated my mind and my emotions. From that moment on, I would never be the same. That smart little boy … the boy who could read 45 rpm record labels with perfect comprehension at an early age died in that bed that morning in September, and another forty-five years would pass before I would find the self-confidence that had been buried in my inner psyche.

I would spend the next forty-five years trying to figure out why I didn't fit in. I would try to figure out what was wrong with me. I would struggle with my gay identity and stumble through what role I was supposed to play in society. I would set myself up to be hurt repeatedly, doing the insane, which was repeating the same actions and expecting a different result. I would allow lust to take me to places that I really shouldn't have gone and mask feelings of inadequacy while all along, searching for the father figure that I needed in my life until I felt like I didn't need it anymore.

With that first touch, I would act out with other little boys until I was whipped to show that the behavior was wrong. And yet no one ever asked me where I learned this from. Not even the psychiatrist that I was dragged to bothered to ask me if I had ever been abused. And you know what? If I had been asked, I may not have answered the question honestly. It wasn't because I needed to hide anything. It wasn't that at all. It was the quiet, unspoken knowledge that what's done in private and in the dark needs to stay private and in the dark.

A child is a very intuitive person. People think that a child doesn't remember the formative years, but it's the formative years that make up the core of us.

Most if not all instances of molestations occur in private: in basements, in bedrooms, in abandoned homes, in attics … any place quiet and out of sight. It doesn't happen in the open where everyone can see. As a result, I believe that a child takes that subliminal message, and it gets stored away in his/her mental Rolodex. If something like this is happening in private, that subconsciously means that I'm supposed to keep this quiet. The abuser doesn't always have to tell you that you have to be quiet. They may mention it to you if they think that you will tell, but in my case, I knew that I wasn't supposed to say anything. I knew that I could never tell my father, not because he would do something to my uncle, but I feared him (my father) as much as I loved him. As a result, I interacted with him in one of two ways: I either worshipped the ground he walked on and behaved as such or lived in fear of his temper. Since what happened to me was pleasurable and done in the dark, I reasoned in my mind not to say anything to anyone, but instead maybe I could recapture those feelings by acting out with other boys. And that's what I did until I got caught.

GETTING CAUGHT

From the moment that a child is touched for sexual gratification, a door is opened that cannot be closed. That child's sense of self has been altered. Who they would have been has been pushed to the back of their mind, and something new is left in its place. Think of it as a drug. You would never give a child a recreational drug. A child, after all, is still learning and is soaking up his/her surroundings. They love their parents and siblings, know that home is safe, and learn to interact with other human beings. In many ways, their senses are on overload. They take in all messages received and process them accordingly. They record both liminal and subliminal messages, and they are all stored in the back of that child's mind.

From the moment that I was kissed by my uncle that night in his bed, something changed in me. In some ways, it was like receiving that first hit of crack, and I wanted to reproduce the sensation it aroused in me. Why wouldn't I? It felt good, and being with another man was natural for me.

Some of you may think that the whole reason why I am gay to this day is because of my introduction to sex at such an early age. I assure you, this is not the case. I would have been gay regardless of my uncle's actions. There are heterosexual men that have been abused by men, and they still love and function very well with women. I've said this before, and I will say it again, being gay is something that you are, not something that you do. It is not about choice. The only choice is when you decide to be true to yourself and admit who you are so that you can live your life in the manner in which you were intended to live it.

We lived in a second-floor apartment above my aunt and uncle related to me on my mother's side of the family. My uncle Lem was my mother's brother, and he and his wife had six children. The oldest of their children was my cousin Charlene that was very close to me in age. In many ways, she was like my younger sister than a cousin, and I loved her dearly. As a matter of fact, I was extremely protective of her. A few of the neighborhood children would come by to play with us, and for the most part, we had a great time.

What stands out in my mind is a light-skinned neighborhood boy whose name escapes me. I'm going to say that I was either eight or nine years of age by this point. Just for the sake of argument, I'll name this boy, Tim. Tim was my height and weight, but he was a handsome kid. He and I fought over my cousin Charlene from time to time, sometimes vying for her attention simultaneously.

What I remember about Tim was his lips. I couldn't tell you what color his eyes were, but I remember he had lips that were over-ripe … like fruit that was ready to be plucked from the vine. I didn't realize that I thought or felt this way about him when I was younger, but hindsight being what it is, I know now that this was the case.

We were playing hide-and-go-seek, and I decided to hide with Tim in the basement. As Charlene counted to ten, Tim and I raced off into the house and hid behind either a stack of boxes or a washing machine in the darkness of the cellar. We didn't turn on the light because we didn't want to be found easily when playing the game.

I didn't realize that this was the perfect environment to recreate the feeling that my uncle had instilled in me. It was dark, we were alone, and I remember that I was the aggressor. In many ways, the basement was the perfect place to hide. You could get lost among the boxes of Christmas decorations and items stored. Normally, my aunt would have the washing machine running, and I would be able to smell the bleach and washing powder. It was in that moment that I kissed Tim completely and unexpectedly. My heart pounded so loud in my chest that I could actually feel it in my ears. Without missing a beat, Tim kissed me back. For a few heart-stopping minutes, it was just me and this boy, his lips pressed against mine.

Now, mind you, I'm not trying to glorify what I was doing or what happened to me in any way, shape, or form. What I'm trying to do is tell you what was going on inside my head at the time. I had forgotten about hide-and-go-seek and was now completely focused on Tim. I was so engrossed that I didn't hear my uncle Lem enter the basement. Tim and I jumped apart at the sound of his voice.

"What are you doing down here?" He stood in the doorway—tall, dark, and imposing.

My response is how most children respond when they are caught doing something that they believe they aren't supposed to be doing.

"Nothing," I said quietly.

"Go on out of here."

Tim and I scurried out of the basement and raced upstairs to the apartment that I lived in. My mother was in the kitchen making dinner. We ran past her and into the living room, the game that we were playing with Charlene long forgotten. At the time, I didn't know if Uncle Lem had actually seen me and Tim kissing. I can only imagine that he did. I was exhilarated. Uncle Lem catching Tim and me had been put far out of my mind. Another thought had taken over. I could feel the same way with this boy that I did with my father's youngest brother. Perhaps, I could even make it last longer.

There was a very small room that sat just off the living room in front of the apartment. There was a small fold-up bed that my father occasionally slept on if he and my mother were fighting. It was on that bed that I unzipped Tim's pants, unzipped my own, and allowed our sexes to touch. I was on top of him, kissing him with a little boy's passion when I heard a gasp from the doorway. My mother stood there, mouth agape. I jumped up with my penis still erect. To this day, I can still see the expression of horror and shock on her face. She ordered Tim out of the house, marched me into the bathroom where there was no place for me to escape. She grabbed an extension cord and whipped me good. I never saw Tim again after that.

Now, I wonder what I would have asked my own son if I caught him doing what she had caught me doing. If I were straight, would I have beaten him, or would I have talked to him to find out where he learned how to do what he was doing? Sadly, if I were a parent in that era, I probably would have beaten him too. Beating is what we knew. That's how we kept our children in line. Now in this day in age, I would hope that I would have the sense to ask my child where he learned how to behave like that. I know now that my kissing Tim came directly from my uncle kissing me. But nobody asked me that. And even if they had, depending on how they asked me, meaning if they demanded me in anger or prodded me with love, it would have a direct impact on the answer that they would have received.

I want you to know that I don't fault my mother at all for her reaction. She reacted in the way that a woman being a product of the '60s would respond. I am sure that she was just as appalled as she was shocked and surprised at my behavior, and the only thing that she could think of at the time was to let me know that my actions were not only unacceptable; they were downright forbidden. Parents didn't ask questions back then. Punishment was swift and painful. This was the old-school mentality. Questions were not asked. Reasoning was not part of the equation. And after that whipping in the bathroom, I knew that I was never to do anything like what I did with Tim again … until I did.

EMOTIONS OUT OF WHACK

My parents fought terribly. As much as I admired my father and tried to please him, I feared him more. His temper would come sometimes without warning, like a twister on an unsuspecting Midwestern town. My mother bore the brunt of his temper though.

I didn't know it then, but he was a misogynist...someone that claimed to love women, but in reality, he loved using them. As much as my mother tried to shield the violence away from me, there were occasions when I heard her being beaten by my father. Nothing could make me cringe more than the sounds of furniture being moved when you knew that it was because your mother's body was being slammed against it. My father and his brothers subscribed to the ideology that if your woman got out of line, it was okay for you to put your hands on them. This was common in the sixties. This was old school, but simply because it was socially acceptable didn't make it right.

Shortly after the birth of my third brother, my parents separated, and the time spent with my father became far and few between. A psychologist once told me that she thought that the reason for my need to be accepted was directly related to the relationship that I had (or didn't have) with my father. I think that she's partially right. Me being a "daddy's boy" and not having him in my life the way that I would have liked definitely impacted my emotional well-being, but not as much as the molestation that changed who I would have been.

I know now that I probably would have been a young boy who would not have craved attention and inclusion as much as I did. The need for attention may have come from the absence of my father, but my need for inclusion came from my molestation. I don't confuse the two, but they are very much entwined. The need for attention is in every child. A child needs to feel as if he/she has worth, especially in the eyes of their parents. If your parents are the first beings that you meet, and you've come to know them as your providers, protectors, and nurturers, why wouldn't their opinion of you matter?

In the same light, if your parents let you down, didn't live up to his/her own expectations, or viewed themselves as failures, what makes you think that this wouldn't impact you as their child? One of the problems that I think we face as a society is that children are growing up too quickly. And because they are growing up at a faster rate than ever before, they are thrust into adult situations without being properly emotionally equipped to handle them. Children may be smart, exude intelligence, and may even look like adults, but believe me, underneath it all, they are still children. And even if they fight it, children still want and need the protection of their parents. It doesn't matter what they say or how they respond to you. Ultimately, what they want is for you to reach out to them in love and foster the trust that's a very necessary ingredient for a healthy relationship.

After my mother left my father, we moved to Philadelphia where we were now surrounded by the support of my mother's family. Periodically, I acted out with other boys, still unaware that I was doing this because of the behavior that had been introduced to me at the age of six. I know that my mother had it rough. She not only had to contend with the fact that she had to raise three boys on her own; she had to deal with the fact that the man she loved was living with another woman, or rather, another woman was living with him. I'm sure that she felt cheated, angry, hurt, and betrayed. She didn't want my father to know where we lived, but eventually, he did find out, and he did come to see us. But that visit didn't lead him to support us financially.

My father popped in on occasion to check in on us initially. And my mother, being who she was, still loved him, even though his behaviors were the reason why she left. We had lived with my aunt and uncle for almost a year in their two-bedroom apartment in Mt. Airy before we found a one-bedroom apartment of our own in North

Philadelphia. When my mother gave birth to my youngest brother, and my father still didn't do anything to support the children that he helped bring into this world, my mother cut him off. I assumed that she felt that as a man, he would never change, and that he would never be the husband and father that she at one time thought that he would be.

The apartment building that we lived in at that time was named Venango Hall, and it held haunting memories for me, first and foremost, because the building was so old, and we lived on the fourth floor. One Halloween, the apartment across from ours caught fire, and the lone occupant had been forced to jump to his death. It used to terrify me to leave and return from school because his apartment door remained opened after the incident, casting an eerie glow on the hallway walls. It was rumored that the man had been smoking in bed, and that he awoke to his apartment engulfed in flames, and when he jumped, he landed on his head. I don't know how true this was, but up until the day we moved to our two-story row home in West Philadelphia, I hated going past the apartment, and I hated that building.

We found a small three-bedroom home in West Philadelphia and moved their promptly. My father had no idea where we were, and I believe that she wanted to keep it that way. Reno Street in many ways was like a miniature family... with all its dysfunctions. I fit in with the boys on the block for the most part, and at this stage of my childhood, things seemed somewhat normal. I had good days, and I had bad days. Reno Street was like an extended family in that everyone knew everyone. What I remember most of all was the way that everyone on the block would turn out if an injustice was being done to any one of us.

There was a woman named Miss Irene, a heavyset, maternal-type of woman who always seemed to have a kind word for everyone that passed her steps. She was dark-skinned, and she almost always wore a headkerchief. When I passed her steps, I always made a point of greeting her with a smile saying, "Hi, Miss Irene." She would always reply in a sweet alto voice, "Hi, darlin'."

Miss Irene had two grown sons, one of which allegedly had mental problems, and one day, she got word that the police had her son cornered on the next block because of an assumed charge that he had assaulted his girlfriend. Miss Irene ran barefoot down the street, and in an instant, word got past from house to house that Miss Irene needed help. People emerged from their homes so quickly that I didn't have time to process what was going on. They followed her, finding her begging the two police officers not to hit her son. And my neighbors surged around those police officers surrounding Miss Irene. It looked like everything was going to get out of hand when just as quickly as the mob (and yes, by this time it was a mob) had formed, they dispersed. Miss Irene was left in tears as they took her son away in a police cruiser. But nobody could tell me then or now that had the neighborhood not come out for her and the police had not taken her son away when they did, there would have been something tantamount to a riot. That's how our neighborhood was back then.

Initially, when we moved to Reno Street, I didn't have a problem fitting in with the other neighborhood boys. It wasn't until I enrolled in parochial school that my social problems began. Or maybe it began long before that, and I just began to notice it when I enrolled in a Catholic school. It doesn't matter what the name of the school is as much as it matters what happened to me while I was there. I had started attending the school in the fifth grade, which I guess would have made me about ten years of age. This school had one grade per group of students, meaning that if you started attending this school with a group of children in grade one, assuming that everyone stayed, you graduated with this same group of children when you finished the eighth grade.

Admittedly, I had problems fitting in with this group of kids. I wasn't an athlete, so playing on the basketball team was out of the question. I wasn't what you would call a "macho" kid. In fact, I was anything but. If someone attacked me verbally, I would simply retreat into myself. It was during this time that my mother took me to several psychiatrists to determine what was wrong with me. It was plain that I didn't behave like a typical boy. In retrospect, I don't think that my behavior wasn't so much out of the norm as it was a reflection of the type of boy that I was. Not every boy is going to be an athlete, but I think in the seventies, that was the expectation. If you didn't play sports, then something was wrong with you. I loved to write. One of my favorite pastimes was to create short stories and cast my friends and family in the starring roles. The closer you were to me emotionally, the bigger the role you had. It was around this time that I thought that something was really wrong with me. I didn't have that sense of belonging that I needed. I tried playing basketball and failed miserably. When the other boys picked teams to play basketball, I was often the last one picked, which drove home the point that I wasn't wanted or needed. I remember carrying around this feeling with me every day. I hated school. Most days seemed to be a struggle for me, and I couldn't understand why.

I found myself being the target of bullies, but ironically, it wasn't from the people that I attended school with. It was from people in my own neighborhood. Sometimes I felt like people could see something in me that translated to it being okay to challenge me. I know now that this wasn't the case. It could be the way that I carried myself... like if you walked with your head down instead of holding it high with confidence. I knew that I didn't have a single confident bone in my body, and on top of it all, I was holding in the secret of me being gay. By now, I knew that I liked boys, but I couldn't bring myself to act on it because it wasn't normal. I repressed those urges by forcing myself to act like other neighborhood boys. I would make catcall noises at the girls because I thought I was supposed to do it. Most times, I had no interest in these girls, but I thought that this was what normal boys did... and above everything, I wanted to be normal.

I remember being invited to a birthday party given by one of my female classmates. I'm pretty sure that it was a birthday party anyway, and I believe that I may have been in the sixth grade at the time. I think that my mother gave me a birthday card and put some money inside to give to the birthday girl. I went to the party and got caught up in the festivities. I saw a beautiful young girl off to the side and thought that this was my chance to go and meet someone who wasn't tainted by the kids that I went to school with. She didn't know that I was a fuckup. She didn't know that I wasn't an athlete. She didn't know anything about me. So after taking a sip of fruit punch, I walked over to her and asked her to dance. She looked at me with a smile and told me no. No? How could she tell me no? I felt like she saw everything inside of me. I thought that she heard every name that I had ever been called. I thought she saw every shortcoming that I had, and without missing a beat, I walked away from her and walked to the edge of the steps that led outside. I had wanted to be accepted, and it didn't work. I felt the tears slide down my face, thinking that maybe pity would win the dance with this pretty girl. It didn't work out that way. Instead, I had embarrassed the birthday girl who told me that she would never invite me to another party of hers as long as she lived. Her mother was understanding and pulled me aside and assured me that everything would be okay.

The thing that I know now is that my need to be accepted was so thrown out of whack, that instead of doing the normal thing and walking away to get some chips and punch or even asking another girl to dance, I took her rejection personally and let it show. I didn't have anyone to lead me or school me in social interaction. Common sense eluded me because I thought that you had to act like a stereotype. It never occurred to me to simply be myself because "myself" at the time was awkward and lacked self-confidence. It was easier to be something that I wasn't because it seemed like that's what everyone else was doing, even if I didn't know this at the time.

Still, I say that when an adult approaches a child for sex, and that first contact is made, that child's emotions are thrown into turmoil and remain like that, even if you as a parent can't see it. My need for inclusion and acceptance was thrown so far out of whack that a simple rejection resulted in me pulling into myself because I had deemed my inner self as safe. I wouldn't hurt me even if other people did. I didn't realize that maybe the trajectory of my emotional well-being would have been a confident young man filled with hopes and promise. Instead, I was on a course that had been altered by my uncle. The cycle had started, and I would be on this roller coaster of emotions for the next few decades.

STAN

I struggled emotionally from the fifth to the eighth grade. My entire time at that elementary school seemed like I was caught in the middle of an ocean amid high waves and gray skies. I would go under only to resurface, gasping for air and then be submerged again. Every now and then, the sun would peek out, and I would have a triumphant moment. Maybe I would sink a basket by accident when playing ball, or I would come to school with a brand-new pair of fashionable shoes and, for a fleeting moment, win the admiration of my classmates. Those experiences were far and few between.

My mother knew that something was wrong, but I believe that she didn't know how to help me. I knew that she wanted to because I was her firstborn son, but sons don't come with instructions or manuals to help fix them in case something goes wrong. She didn't have the assistance of my father to intervene in this situation, not that he would have known what to do if he could. As I said before, my parents came from the old school, where the answer to a child that was a disciplinary problem was to beat or punish them. And it wasn't that this was necessarily a bad idea, but looking back on it now, I think that it was a simple answer to a complex problem. Now don't get me wrong, many kids could benefit from a good old-fashioned ass whipping. In fact, if there were a bit more of those ass whippings administered when needed, kids probably wouldn't be as out of control as they are today. But that's just my opinion.

My mother took me to at least three psychiatrists that I can remember. The first one was a white man with a large behind that asked me on my first visit if I knew what "effeminate" was.

I told him that it was when a boy acted like a girl.

He said to me, "Well, your mother thinks that you're effeminate."

I don't remember going back to see him again.

I realize now that it wasn't so much that I was effeminate as I was just different. Back then, a boy being different often translated to him being gay. If you were an introvert, you were gay. If you weren't aggressive, you were gay. If you preferred reading to playing sports, you were gay. It seemed that the worst thing that you could call a boy in the seventies was gay ... and believe me, I had that name thrown at me quite often. I firmly believe that when a male child displayed behaviors that were deemed as out of the norm for a boy, he was labeled gay. But it wasn't so much that he displayed homosexual tendencies as it was that most people didn't know what they were seeing when the child didn't behave like a "typical" boy.

I think that what made matters worse for me was that I was trying so hard to keep that secret about me out of plain sight, but it seemed like everyone could see it in me, and I didn't know what to do about it. The only solution that came to mind was to date girls, but I didn't know how. I had no one to tell me how to interact with girls, and when I think about it, there really was no reason for me to have been entertaining the notion of dating girls. I was ten, eleven, and twelve. To my knowledge, ten-, eleven-, and twelve-year-olds didn't date. But I didn't know that at the time. I only knew what the other boys were doing (or saying that they were doing.)

When I reached the seventh grade, I remember that some of my classmates and a few of the boys in the eighth grade would go to dinner and the movies with a young man named Stan. Stan was in his early thirties, old enough to be my father, and I wanted to go. I wanted to go with my classmates and enjoy the company of this older man. My mother told me no immediately. To her, something wasn't right about a man in his thirties spending so much free time with young boys when none of them were his own children. My mother's instincts were dead-on, but it didn't matter to me. I would hear the boys talk about going to the movies to see Bruce Lee movies or going to dinner at Paganos, one of the more upscale Italian restaurants in

West Philly at the time. Once again, I felt left out…like I wasn't good enough to go.

Looking back, I know now that me feeling like I wasn't good enough was another by-product of being molested at such a young age.

I wanted to belong. I wanted to be included for once. And I'll be honest with you; Stan was a very handsome man. He was African American, dark-skinned, tall, solid…the ideal candidate for the father figure that I was seeking. He was funny. I would see him occasionally in passing with the other boys, and he always seemed to have them laughing, and I wanted to belong.

I pleaded with my mother to let me go, and eventually, she let me. I had joined the "Woodshop" team. It was held at night in the upper portion of the church. We were taught the fine art of wood craftsmanship. But because it was held so late, we all needed a ride home, and that's where Stan came in. If it was early enough, he would take us all out to dinner. We loved it, and our parents probably enjoyed getting us out of the house and having innocent fun with each other. I was finally part of the "in" crowd. And that's when I noticed Stan…I mean, *really* noticed him. I wanted to be close to him. I wanted to be like a son to him. I was allowed to go out on more and more excursions, and the more I went, the more I wanted to spend time with Stan.

Eventually, he took notice of me, and I was elated. He made sure that when we went to the movies, I sat directly beside him. When he dropped us off at home, I was the last boy to be dropped off. This slowly evolved into me spending more time with him without the other boys, and I felt special.

On some Saturdays, I would go over and help him wash his car. At the time, he had two vehicles: a huge station wagon that he would use to take all of us boys to and from our destinations and a bright orange Volkswagen Beetle.

When I helped him wash the cars, it was so much like a father and son experience that I was on emotional overload. It was like all the television shows that depicted father and sons. We laughed like no tomorrow, and I started feeling things about him…things that

I wasn't sure of at first. I wanted him for myself. I wanted him to continue playing the fantasy role of my absentee father. I say fantasy because that's exactly what it was. It was the good parts of parenthood with none of the bad. There was no discipline … only love and fun. If things could have continued like this, I would have been the happiest boy in the world. But things changed. Not immediately and not overnight. When I look back on all this, I know now that I was being groomed, and that it wouldn't be too much longer before Stan would make his intentions known.

Men, as a rule, don't like classifying themselves as victims. Boys are brought up to be strong. We are reared to be protectors of our women, children, and homes. We are taught to be fearless in the face of adversity, and there's nothing wrong with that. But being a victim is not a virtue. We consider it a weakness, and because of that, we remain silent. We don't talk about the occasions where we are victims; but just because we don't talk about it doesn't make us any less a victim.

Heterosexual men respond differently to molestation than gay men respectively. But individually, each man reacts in a way that coincides with his nature as well as what was physically done to him. I am not a licensed psychologist, but I believe that if a man who identifies himself as a heterosexual is violated by another man as a child, his response may be anger first and foremost because engaging in sex with another man is not in his nature. He is literally being forced to do something that he does not want to do and feels powerless to stop it. This is true even if he gets an erection or experiences an orgasm. This may create feelings of helplessness and conflict, followed by anger; but as a child, you may not know the reason why. You may not necessarily be emotionally equipped to connect the dots. The molester may use the fact that the child's body responding to the sexual event as the child being a willing participant. He may even tell the child that you wanted this to happen, and you liked it, so this makes you just as guilty as me. Back in the seventies, a boy did not want to be considered gay, so they kept their mouths closed and didn't say anything, allowing the molestation to continue.

A homosexual man may respond completely different to being molested by another man. For gay men, sleeping with men is natural. Having sex with an adult man may even be construed as a badge of honor. It would be no different than a heterosexual boy having sex with an adult woman.

But simply because a boy has sex with an adult, whether that adult is male or female, the fact remains that an adult is having sex with a child, and it doesn't matter if that child gives their consent or not. The adult is in control. They know better and should exercise restraint and self-control.

We know that children don't look like children nowadays. We know that children are physically maturing at a faster rate than just twenty years ago. But simply because a child physically looks like an adult doesn't make them an adult. That child isn't capable of making a decision such as consenting to indulge in a sexual act with an adult. They are not emotionally equipped do so. They think they are, but they aren't. Anyone below the age of fourteen doesn't understand the ramifications of sex. All they know is that it feels good.

And as for the adult, all they know is that it feels good to them even if it doesn't to the child. In their mind, they think that the child will ultimately forget what is being done to them. They may convince themselves that the child is enjoying the act just as much as they are, and that the enjoyment translates to no emotional damage being done. They couldn't be more wrong.

THE CHAIR AGAINST THE DOOR

The first thing that I noticed about Stan's home was that it was quiet... I mean really quiet. I knew that his elderly mother and brother lived there, but neither of them was home at the time. The house was a two-story row home decorated with furnishings that looked as if they would be more at home in an antique store than in someone's house. When you entered the house, you walked through a small living room decorated in drab greens and brown tones. To the left was the carpeted stairs that led to the second floor, and to the right stood the entryway to the dining room. They didn't have any pets of any kind. In retrospect, maybe the reason why it was so quiet was so if anyone came in, he would be able to hear them. I'll never know if this was the actual reason. All I remember is that Stan's room was in the back of the house at the top of the stairs, and honestly, I didn't think twice about going up there with him. We had just washed his car, and he paid me five dollars. In the seventies, five dollars went far. Consider the fact that bus fare at the time was only thirty-five cents... forty if you needed a transfer. Penny candy cost an actual penny, and a pack of Now and Later was a nickel.

Once we got upstairs to his room, I was struck by how small it was. The room was dominated by a full-sized bed. He had a wooden hard-backed chair that he placed in front of the bedroom door after closing it behind us. He had wedged the back of the chair underneath the door handle, and once again, I didn't think anything of it.

Stan wasn't an overly muscular man, but he was big in stature. I felt safe with him. Being alone with him in this small enclosed space didn't alarm me. In fact, it did the total opposite. He took off his shirt and stood before me with that disarming smile. I didn't realize it at the time, but this was part of the grooming process. Grooming a child for sex includes many tactics, and they vary from perpetrator to perpetrator, but the result is the same. The abuser wants to gain the child's trust. They have to manipulate that child into consenting to be touched, perhaps influencing them into thinking that the idea of sex was their idea. I remember feeling glad that I was finally alone with him and that I had the father figure that I desperately needed. He stood in front of me, looking down at me with soft brown eyes.

"I'm glad you're here. You know that?" he said as he settled on the edge of his bed and slowly began to remove his sneakers.

"Yeah." I smiled while sitting down beside him. "I'm glad to be here too."

"Did you have fun today? I mean, washing the car. I appreciate it."

I nodded, watching him as he slid his socks off his feet, and then seemingly without thought, he draped his arm around my shoulders. I felt my heart rate increase. He was touching me. I mattered. I actually mattered to an older man who wanted to look out for me.

"Stan?" I said in a small voice.

"Hmmmm?"

I didn't know how I was going to ask him the question that had been bubbling in my mind for a few days now.

"Can I ask you something?" I began.

"You can ask me anything." He reclined back onto the bed, stretching his body before me. "Get comfortable. It's just you and me now," he said.

I took off my shirt, shoes, and sneakers and then stretched out beside him. He was on his side, and as I faced him, I realized that now was the time for me to ask him the question that almost petrified me to let fall from my lips. I knew that if his answer wasn't what I wanted it to be, I would be crushed.

"Would you ... would you be my dad? I mean, would you—"

"You want me to be your father?"

There it was ... out in the open. I wanted to take it back but couldn't. It was so quiet in the room ... quiet enough that I could hear my heart pounding in my ears. And then he reached out to me, pulling me close to him in a warm embrace. I was safe. He wouldn't hurt me, and finally, there was a man in my life who would protect me. There was someone that I could go to just in case life got too rough for me. He held me close and kissed me lightly on the forehead.

"Yes," he said softly. "I'll be your father. I would be honored to call you my son."

I released my breath as I buried my head in his chest, taking in his scent. He smelled like Hai Karate Aftershave and sweat. I had asked the question that I had been dying to ask him for weeks, and he had given me the answer that I had wanted to hear. I hugged him tightly, feeling my eyes welling up with tears ... tears that I wouldn't let fall. I knew that he cared about me, but I didn't know how deep it went.

Still, I didn't know this at the time, but I would find out years later that Stan had done this before ... many, many times before. I wasn't the first boy that he had in his room, and I wouldn't be the last. As a result, he had honed his grooming skills. We were alone, so I knew that this time was exclusively ours. As he stood before me without a shirt, I now understand that he was sending unspoken signals. Our friendship was shifting. When he stretched his body out on the bed, it was another signal. If I had not picked up on the signal, he would have done something else to send another signal, indicating that it was okay for me to touch him. In many ways, it was like playing a game of checkers; he would do something to prompt me to make a move. If I didn't take the hint, he would do something else. It could be something as simple as taking off his shoes and socks to further undress himself in front of me. But the thing that I understand now about him was that I had to be the aggressor, not him. If I made the move, then it would buy my silence. After all, a boy would be more likely to keep quiet if he thought that he was in control of the situation and coerced the adult into sex, even if it was really the adult manipulating the child.

We didn't have sex that day. We were still in the grooming process because now the idea had been planted. Seeing him in only a pair of jeans now put the idea of sex in my mind. Now going to his room held a different allure. I was making the mental connection with what happened to me years before. There was the strong possibility that I could feel good with a man that I idolized. It didn't matter that he was old enough to be my father, and I never thought for a moment that he was controlling me. The chair against the door wasn't being used to keep me in as much as it was being used to keep people out for a reason.

On the night of our first encounter, I was one of the last boys to be dropped off after an evening out with my classmates. Instead of him taking me home, we stopped by his house, and as usual, no one was home.

There are three things that I remember about that night: (1) The chair was placed against the door as usual. (2) The room was deafeningly quiet … I mean, so quiet that I thought that I could hear bells ringing. I didn't realize that it was the silence ringing in my ears. (3) I had been manipulated to kiss him for the first time.

I think it's important for you to know that I don't blame anyone for this. I don't blame my mother, my absentee father, or even my uncle that molested me that first time so many years ago. For years, I thought that things just happened, and that they happen for a reason. I wouldn't find out for another forty-five years just what psychological damage had been done by all these events. I can try to claim ownership for some of the circumstances that occurred in my life, but the truth is that at age six, thirteen, and fourteen … you can't. That would be like a police officer blaming the rape victim for being raped.

Molestation is about a pedophile that seeks gratification by having sex with children. Sometimes, it matters what the sex of the victim is; sometimes it doesn't. The first and primary criterion that has to be met is that the victim has to be a child. After that condition is met, it simply becomes a matter of what sex the pedophile prefers. I believe that there are varying degrees of pedophiles. There are ones that like to manipulate their victims passively, such as Stan. They're the ones that like to take the direct approach and simply make their intentions known from the very beginning, and then there are the ones that like to dominate and intimidate their victims by brute force.

I've only met two out of the three. I've never been dominated by force that I can remember. And I guess because of that, I just assumed that no damage has been done. No one had ever hurt me … not physically anyway.

But emotional damage had been done, but because I couldn't see it, I couldn't acknowledge it, and if I couldn't acknowledge it, then I couldn't fix it. As a result, I believe that I lived forty-five of my fifty-one years in the dark.

WHAT GOES ON IN THE MIND OF AN ABUSED CHILD?

One of the things that I knew from the moment of that first touch was that it wasn't traumatic. It wasn't as if my uncle physically violated me. What I believe is that the way a child's mind processes what has happened to him or her runs in direct correlation to how painful or brutal the experience was at the time. A child's senses are new as they become acclimated to their surroundings. If the experience was pleasant, it's like giving a child a piece of candy. If left to their own devices, a child would eat candy until either an adult tells them not to, or they got physically ill from overindulgence.

Sex is no different. A child knows pleasure, but they cannot decipher how to moderate it. They rely on their parental figures to do that for them. Pleasure can come in the form of candy, good food, movies, sports, or whatever the child enjoys doing. Children enjoy going out to play, but every adult knows that they cannot do it every minute of every day of their lives, or there will be consequences. Children love candy, but every adult knows that a child cannot live off a diet of candy because it would be detrimental to their health if they did so.

Sex is normal when it happens within the time frame that it is supposed to happen. But when it happens too soon, it changes the child. Since sex with a child happens in secret and if the event was pleasurable, the child may place himself or herself in situations where molesters can and oftentimes will take advantage of them. They may know that it is wrong for them to behave the way that they are behaving, but they do it because they don't know any better, thus continuing the cycle of molestation.

In my case, I was looking for a father figure until I grew old enough to not need one as badly as I thought that I did. This may explain why the abuse stopped when I got into my midteens.

The thing that people don't understand with a victim is that they don't know how to handle the repercussions of sex at an early age. They don't regard it as something that is being done to them. They may even look at it as a way of feeling good for the moment. Add to the mix that a boy going into his teens is ready physically for sexual activity. Their hormones are kicking in. They may feel like they're ready for sex even if they aren't.

For victims of molestation where the abuse was traumatic, this demographic may develop trust issues with people in general and the sex of their abuser in particular. Men who may have had trauma inflicted on them by an abuser may experience anger and rage. As they grow older, they may experience bouts of depression without knowing why. They may think that there is something wrong with them, which may lend itself to drug and alcohol abuse. In the same breath, women may develop deep-seated feelings of anger mixed with the inability to trust anyone around them. Like their male counterparts, they may develop problems with alcohol and drugs in an attempt to mask whatever pain they may be trying to quell. They may look for relief in anything or anyone that they can. In some instances, they may numb themselves to what has happened, and in that numbing process make it difficult for anyone to get to know them to establish a normal sense of intimacy.

Everyone's circumstance is unique to themselves, and there is no one-size-fits-all answer to this problem. While I will never blame the victim of abuse for what has happened to them, it is important to know what occurs in the cycle of abuse and how it continues to perpetuate itself.

Stan gave me everything that I thought I wanted at the time of my encounters with him. He knew I wanted a father. This may explain how he managed to target boys whose fathers weren't present. He gave me gifts to earn my trust, thus buying my silence. I believe that although he didn't have to do this, he did it to ensure my cooperation. Nothing could be left to chance. He needed me to be willing, and I was, even if I didn't know that what was happening to me was wrong. I believe that to break this cycle, parents and parental figures need to pay attention to their children. Children will not make it easy for you to do so. Most will even protect their abuser in the hopes of protecting their "special" relationship in order for the abuse to continue. This is perhaps the most difficult part of a parent's role when it comes to protecting their children. How do you get your child to talk to you honestly about something that they may feel too embarrassed to share with you?

There is no easy answer to this because we are living in an age now where because of technology, children have access to graphic images of adults doing things that they cannot understand. In the seventies, there was no Internet. Kids relied on learning about sex either through friends, classmates, or the occasional candid discussion with a parent. Now, with the click of a button, a child can access porn on their laptops, tablets, or phones. They can go to a friend's house and watch it on cable television.

So what went on in my mind during the periods of abuse? When it happened with my uncle, it was pleasure. It was in this pleasure that I acted out with the occasional neighborhood boy. When I turned thirteen, what I missed most was my father figure. More than anything, at that point in time, I wanted an adult male to take an interest in me. I wanted the images that I saw on television when Father's Day would roll around. I wanted to do the things with a man that a father and son should be doing. Sex was not in the equation. That didn't come until I met an adult male that wanted that from me.

In my mind, I thought that the trade-off would be fair. He would be there to protect me. He would be there to be my comforter and confidant. But he could also make me feel good physically. He would be responsible for making me have an orgasm. This was not the norm but an exception. When Mr. Jackson molested me, I didn't feel like I had the right to say no. I didn't want him to be my father, and I certainly had no desire for him. I let it happen because deep down inside, I thought that as my homeroom teacher, I didn't have a choice. I reasoned that if I found him remotely attractive, I would have liked it, so I simply let it happen. But I'm getting ahead of myself.

The grooming process can be as long or as short as the molester wants it to be. It depends on the psyche of the child. What occurs during the grooming process is the establishment of trust between the victim and the abuser. Once that trust is there, it will be difficult for the child to turn on his or her molester and tell someone, because most of the time, they don't even realize that something is being done to or taken away from them. This makes the parents' role all the more difficult should the child start exhibiting behaviors that may be out of character or the norm for them.

As someone just going into their teens, no matter what anyone tells you, that child cannot give consent. They simply aren't emotionally able to do so. They don't have the capacity to think about the long-term effects. They don't even realize that something is being done *to* them. Instead, they think that because it feels good, they are willing participants.

Crazy, right?

WAS I THAT OBVIOUS?

The affair with Stan didn't go on for a long time, but it felt like it did. My mother knew that something was wrong, but she couldn't put her finger on it. I believe that her parental instincts kicked in, and she felt that not only was something wrong with a grown man wanting to spend all his free time with young boys; she felt like something was wrong with this man wanting to spend so much of his free time with *her* boy. But because I felt so strongly about Stan, I defended him fiercely, denying any allegations that she may have made.

By now, I was in the eighth grade, and I was really struggling, both socially and academically. My eighth-grade teacher was a nun that had just come from the south, and what I believe now is that our personalities simply didn't mesh. In the one year that I had been in her class, I was suspended and sent to the principal's office more times than I had in the entire four years that I had been attending this particular parochial school. I did not have the foresight to equate my academic struggles with my sexual relationship with Stan.

The last and final incident that involved me and this teacher resulted in a parent-teacher conference where my mother had to come up to the school. My mother, the principal, my teacher, and I were in attendance. I don't remember every single detail of the meeting... only the highlights. The principal was stern in telling my mother that she had to stop making unsubstantiated allegations about Stan. My teacher stated that I never did my homework. My mother asked me if this was true, and my response was, "Mom, I did do my homework." This infuriated my teacher, and she said in a voice laced with anger, "Jerome Whitehead, you're going to fail!"

Now the truth of the matter was that neither she nor I were accurate. She alleged that I never did my homework, and I said that I did. I did my homework... most of the time. Honestly, why I did it on some occasions and not others remains a mystery to me. I can only attribute it to me being socially challenged, not liking my environment and the molestation that I was going through but struggling to keep hidden.

My mother took this statement from my teacher to mean that no matter what I did, she was going to leave me behind to repeat the eighth grade again. With just a few months before graduating to the ninth grade, my mother pulled me out of the school and placed me in a school in North Philadelphia. She didn't want her child to be left behind, and she wanted me to continue on to high school. I think at that point, she could see that there was a personality conflict between me and the teacher.

But with that transfer came something more than what I could have ever bargained for. And at age thirteen, I had unknowingly stumbled into another circumstance that would chip away at what little bit of innocence that I had left.

It was also around this time that I discovered a safety net that I would later parlay into the man that I ultimately would become. I began to write. I found that it was easier to create my own worlds with pen and paper than it was to exist on my own. Writing became my go-to when things got out of hand or became too much for me to bear. Sometimes, I would go to the movies and see a film that I enjoyed, and then go home and take the same plot but change the characters to include myself, family, and friends. This worked for the longest time and provided me with a huge sense of amusement. I could create societies and circumstances where I fit in and wasn't awkward. In my stories, I was popular and could control the situation at hand. In my stories, I wasn't a victim, I wasn't awkward, and I didn't have any underlying issues with men or boys. I had a girlfriend who loved me, and I loved her, and we had other couples that were included in our inner circle. I created these stories for quite some time, and for a while, they worked, and I was okay. But life has an unusual way of getting in the way, and sooner or later, I would find out that pen and paper wouldn't do.

I am purposely not naming any of the schools that I went to because I don't feel like it's necessary. I also think that the details that I am providing to describe the incidents of molestation are appropriate because it lends credence as to why I behaved the way that I did.

Going to another school and starting over was good ... at least in the beginning. I didn't feel like I belonged at the parochial school that I had just left, and to be honest with you, I was more excited about meeting new students than I was about acknowledging missing my emotional connection to Stan. I didn't know it at the time, but Stan had moved on to another boy. It would be a few years later before I would find this out.

The school that I had moved to was predominately black with a quarter of the students belonging to other races. Up until then, I had never met other children from other races, and the differences between us culturally fascinated me. But while I looked forward to going to a new school, I was also terrified. What if the new students viewed me as my old classmates did? What if they could see my character flaws and weaknesses?

You see, this is what molestation does to a child. Even if the event is pleasurable, it takes away your self-esteem. You're not allowed to grow into the human being that you were destined to be. That confident person has been pushed to the back of your mind, and what's left in the forefront is who you are now ... a person that thinks about sex almost constantly and, for the most part, whose value is now wrapped up in that. You forget that you are smart, attractive, and intelligent. As you go into adolescence, your hormones begin to kick in, but it only adds to the emotional confusion because at the same time that you are craving what was done to you in private, you also know that it is wrong. You're at war with yourself even if you don't know it. This isn't the story for everyone, but I believe that it is like that for many of us.

I stood outside of my new homeroom, knowing that it was full of students who would either like me or not. What if they liked me? What if they didn't? I must have stood in the hallway for a good five minutes before I placed my hand on the doorknob. I took a deep breath and entered the classroom not knowing what to expect. What I got was something that I could never have anticipated... They applauded.

"Potential" by the Jimmy Castor Bunch, "Free Man" by the South Shore Commission, and "Ease on Down the Road" by Consumer Rapport were the popular songs being played on the radio at the time. My homeroom teacher was an older black man, probably about fifty-five years of age. As I walked into the room and took a seat, I thought that everything was going to be okay. For the first time in years, I felt normal. I didn't feel like an outsider. I didn't feel a desire for men. I didn't even miss Stan. I was so engrossed in my new surroundings that all I wanted to do was make new friends. I made friends quickly. But even more importantly, I was experiencing something that was also new to me. I was popular. Some of the girls actually thought that I was cute. I couldn't believe it. I didn't understand what they were seeing. But whatever the case, I was content with my surroundings.

My homeroom teacher's name was Mr. Jackson, and many of the students thought that he was the coolest teacher around. He was older than the average teacher, but he had a no-nonsense way about him. He had a short Afro, thick graying mustache, and had a lean build. In many ways, he was very street savvy, using the language that most kids could relate to. I thought that Mr. Jackson was cool initially, and I assumed that he thought the same thing about me.

During assembly, he would make sure that I occupied the seat next to him. And during whatever presentation that would be made, I became aware of where he placed his hand. It was too close to mine. What I mean is that, it was almost as if he was trying to place his hand in mine. I dismissed it the first time that this happened, but after a couple of assemblies, I noticed the pattern, and I became uncomfortable. Mr. Jackson wasn't like Stan. Where I felt myself attracted to Stan, I felt no attraction to Mr. Jackson at all.

It was common for us to have a recess break right after we finished lunch. Most times, we would go outside to play wall ball, or the girls would jump rope. Mr. Jackson called me into the school during recess. The reason was that he wanted to tutor me in reading. I had no problem in reading. As a matter of fact, reading and spelling was my strongest subject. Once alone in the homeroom class, he would close the door, sit close to me, and open up a book. He would ask me to read a chapter, which I did without a problem. But while I was reading, I noticed that his hand would wander close to me ... close to my hand, close to my leg ... and I would move away from him. He would counter by moving closer to me.

He finally looked at me and asked me, "Do you talk?"

I remember looking back at him and replying, "Sure, I talk. Don't all kids talk?"

I didn't understand what he meant until he slid his hand up my thigh and caressed it. How did he know? Was I that obvious? How did he know that this happened to me before? Was there something in me that was plainly visible? Was it possible that I really was effeminate and just didn't know it? All these questions swirled around in my mind as the days passed by.

Mr. Jackson eventually took me to the teacher's lounge on one of the upper floors of the school. After locking the door behind us, he unzipped my pants and did the same with himself and then inserted his sex into my zipper. I remember wondering why he didn't have an erection, and as we stood against the wall, he gyrated, moving back and forth until he had an orgasm inside of my pants.

I remember reasoning with myself about what had happened. I didn't like it, but I thought that there were worse things that could have happened to me. Besides, if Mr. Jackson were attractive, it wouldn't have been so bad, and I probably would have enjoyed the experience. I didn't know that I wasn't supposed to rationalize this way.

I remember trying to tell my mother about what was happening, but I didn't know how because it was embarrassing. I told her that Mr. Jackson was too close to me. I didn't know how to tell her that he actually felt my leg or any other parts of my body. She said that he probably felt like a father to me since she knew that he had kids of his own.

But the funny thing about all this is that from the moment that Mr. Jackson started molesting me is right about the time when some of the attitudes that my classmates about me began to change. I didn't know what it was, but all of a sudden, it felt like it did at my old school. I felt like I was on the outskirts again. I was glad that I didn't have to spend years with these kids like I did at my old school.

I never regarded sex with Mr. Jackson, Stan, or my uncle for that matter as a problem. Maybe I should have. But that's the problem with children that have sex too soon. As a child, you don't know how you're supposed to feel. You don't know anything outside of what your body is telling you. If being touched by someone that you are remotely attracted to feels good, then you're probably going to go along with it, not knowing that there are/will be repercussions for those actions. I knew what society said I was supposed to be. I knew how people said I was supposed to behave. And maybe that was part of the problem to begin with. In order to know how to behave, you need a role model to emulate. Every boy needs a man to look up to ... someone that will lead his family and guide his son into manhood. Sadly, many boys don't have this, and as a result, too many people, places, and things will jump in to take the place of the absentee father.

I met Dina Mariano in my algebra class. I noticed her the way that a boy would notice the "new" girl that just arrived at his school. Her long dark hair flowed down her back until it almost touched her waist. She was full figured, voluptuous in a way that a fifteen-year-old girl had no business being at that age. I was drawn to her not just because she was beautiful; that would have been easy. But what I saw in her eyes when she caught me looking at her was a look that every boy hopes to see when he looks at a pretty girl. She was smiling back at me. I wasn't used to this. Pretty girls ... white, black, or otherwise didn't look at me. And so I did the only thing that I knew to do in that situation. I passed her a note with my name on it. I already knew her name, but I had to ask her again. When class was over, she met me in the hallway.

"Dina," she said with a smile.

Her eyes were dark brown, and she wore a nude lip gloss that made her lips look so inviting. She wore light makeup with just a hint of green/blue eye shadow. I looked at her up and down, trying to think of something to say.

"Do you have a name?" she asked. "We have to get to the next class, so you better hurry up."

"Jerome," I said with a smile while extending my hand to her. "Can I... carry your books?"

She smiled, and it was like someone had turned on the sun inside my heart.

"What's your next class?" she asked while handing me her books, piling them on top of my own.

I thought for a moment. I couldn't remember.

"You kids better get on to your next class," I heard a voice over my left shoulder.

"Sure, Mr. Jackson."

Dina looked over my shoulder at the same time that I turned around to see my homeroom teacher looking at the both of us. I glanced at Mr. Jackson who looked at us with a look that I couldn't make out at first.

"Let's go, Jerome," she said as we started down the hallway. And thus, the romance began.

As the days became weeks, Dina and I began to date ... or at least, in my mind, we did. She had brought me home to meet her mother who was thrilled to meet me. She thought that I was well-mannered and probably age appropriate for her daughter. I didn't realize at that time that Dina had more than one boyfriend. We never talked about being exclusive; I just assumed that we were. But time has a weird way of doing things to a perceived relationship, and in retrospect, Dina probably thought that I was "moving" too slow. I was still a virgin ... at least as far as sleeping with a woman was concerned, and I didn't know what to do with a girl if I ever came across one to do anything with.

There was something about Dina that held a special allure for me. It was more than just the way that she tossed her hair over her shoulders whenever she talked to me. It was more than the way she looked at me that gave me a window into her thoughts. She had a way of turning my insides to melted butter when she would run her index finger across the palm of my hand before holding it. I wondered if this was what dating a girl was supposed to be like. Was this the way I was supposed to feel? I mean, at this point, all I had to compare what I was feeling to was the movies.

On the day that Dina left a note on my algebra textbook asking me to come by her house after school, I was filled with mixed emotions. She made it a point of telling me in her note that nobody would be home. And when school let out, I couldn't get to her house fast enough.

Spring was slowly gliding into summer, and as I made my way to Dina's house, I remember the sun beating down on me, causing the sweat to run down the sides of my face. My shirt clung to my back, and I remember feeling butterflies in my stomach as I knocked on her front door. She opened it with a smile and asked me to come in.

"Would you like something to drink?" she asked as she entered the living room.

"Sure." I smiled at her as she walked through the house into the kitchen.

I followed her as we crossed the dining room with the overly large rectangular wooden table that dominated the area. Dina's kitchen was small and sat at the opposite end of the house. As she approached the doorway that led into the kitchen, a man turned the corner and glanced at her with a slight smile. He was light-skinned black, relatively tall with a full mustache that sat above thick lips. He was long muscled, wearing what initially appeared to be a policeman's uniform. For a moment, we just looked at each other. He looked like he was in his early twenties. It never occurred to me to wonder why he was hanging around with a teenage girl.

"Jerry, this is Zeke." Dina passed by him and then disappeared into the kitchen. "Zeke, this is Jerry."

Zeke smiled at me and extended his hand. I took it, but the look on my face must have conveyed what I felt. I was confused.

"Hi," I mumbled.

"Dina told me about you." He smiled while releasing my hand slowly.

Dina returned from the kitchen with a glass of water and handed it to me. I took it and almost drained the glass of its contents in a single gulp.

Zeke looked at me with soft brown eyes, and then he turned his attention back to Dina.

"Can you let me talk to him for a minute?" he asked softly.

"What?" She glanced at me and then back at him. I don't think this was the reaction that she expected from him.

"Can you give us a second?" he asked, only the tone of his voice had taken on more of a stern edge.

Dina turned abruptly and marched into the living room, leaving us alone in the dining room.

"Come into the kitchen with me." He turned and disappeared through the narrow doorway.

I finished my water hoping that it would wash down the lump that had suddenly appeared in my throat. In that instant, everything became clear. Zeke was her boyfriend, and for some reason, she wanted me to meet him. I had always known that certain types of girls could be vindictive, although for the life of me, I didn't know why. I could understand if I did something to hurt her, but in this instance, I hadn't done anything to Dina. The only thing that I could think of was that she wanted to show me that she could do better by landing herself a man instead of a boy. Now I was standing in a tiny kitchen with the heat of the day, making it feel more like a closet.

"I know you like her," he began in a gentle voice. "You do like her, don't you?"

I nodded my head and then looked up at him. His dark-brown Afro was only three inches in length.

"I'm sorry." He looked at me, almost as if he was looking through me.

"You didn't do anything." I looked away from him. All I wanted to do was leave. What was the point in me staying?

"It's going to be all right," he said.

My feelings began to tumble inside of me and began to feel myself getting angry. It was time to go home. We both heard the slam of the front door and realized that Dina had stormed out of the house. Why she was angry was beyond me.

"How do you feel?" he asked me.

"I don't know," I said as the anger began to course through me.

"Sorry." He looked down at the floor. "She shouldn't have brought you here... not like this." And then he pulled me close to him and hugged me tight.

My body went rigid.

"This won't happen to you again." I heard him say softly.

❧

There are many gay men that say that they knew they were gay from a very early age. I believe this to be true, myself included, even if they don't know exactly what being gay is at that time. The problem is that with the stigma of what being gay meant at the time (and to a degree what it still means in society today), no one in his right mind would want to own that. Man, being the social creature that he is, wants to belong, and for me, this was exacerbated to the tenth power. I had no interest in being estranged from my limited social circles. I wanted to belong to something. I couldn't figure out what it was about me that made grown men think that it was okay to approach me.

I wanted to be straight. I wanted to be like every other boy out there minus the sports. There were girls that I certainly found attractive, and at the time, I thought that if I met the right girl, I could perhaps live a normal life. But I guess you have to first determine what is normal since what is deemed as normal for one may not be deemed as normal for another. As quickly as my relationship with Dina started, it had ended.

What took its place was my unexpected friendship with Ezekiel Price. He began meeting me after school, and we would grab a soda or a burger at a nearby McDonald's. Zeke told me that he was a cop, but after hanging around him, I realized that he really wanted to be a police officer; I just didn't know it at the time. The thing is, I actually liked Zeke. He was funny, smart … and somehow, he knew how to get to me. He was old enough to be my older brother, and in some weird way, I looked up to him. He came off as protective. And yet I couldn't tell him about what was happening with me and Mr. Jackson. Dina began to fade into the background as my friendship with Zeke intensified. I didn't know if he was dating her or not. In my mind, it didn't matter. She wanted me to meet the man that she was messing around with without regard to my feelings. In my mind, she was no better than the girls that I had left behind in the elementary school back in West Philly.

And like Stan, Zeke had become a male figure that I could look up to. He gave me the attention that I needed while focusing his attention on me … and for a few short weeks, all was right with the world. I didn't know what Zeke really wanted from me. I can't feign 100 percent innocence with what happened between Zeke and me. Since I had been groomed, I knew what to expect from certain types of men. Stan had taught me well. There is an unspoken form of communication that occurs between a child that has been groomed and molested. If the initial form of molestation wasn't traumatic, then it makes it easier for the child to understand the language that occurs when they meet another adult who takes an interest in them. And while we're on the subject of Stan, I wouldn't find out until a few years later that he had moved on to another friend of mine who was in the seventh grade. When he had done this, I have no idea, but clearly, this was a pattern with him. If something happened with one boy, whether they graduated or his mother objected to the personal attention that Stan paid to her child, he would simply move on to someone else.

As I stated earlier, Zeke used to meet me after school and would walk me to the subway station. Sometimes we would grab something quick to eat, or we would go back to his house and hang out for a while. Zeke didn't cross any major lines with me in my mind until the day of a school trip. I will never, ever forget this trip.

Summer was rapidly approaching, and today, it was hot…hotter than I thought it should be for late spring, but it was perfect for a school outing to Great Adventure. We had gone through the African safari on a rental bus that looked like it had at one time belonged to Continental Trailways or Greyhound.

It was late when we got back. The sun had just begun to set when I got off the bus just in time to see Zeke waiting for me in front of the school. He was leaning against the building, and when he saw me, he smiled.

"Hey," he said while sidling up beside me. "So how was the trip?"

"It was good." I looked up at him as all my classmates began to make their way home.

"Do you have some time to stop by my house for a little while?"

I looked at the sun as it began to set in the sky, bathing the neighborhood in dwindling gold and yellow sunshine. It would be dark soon.

"I don't know, Zeke. I should be getting home. It's getting dark."

"It won't be that long." He looked down at me and smiled. It was disarming, charming…warm and inviting. "I promise, it's just for a couple of minutes."

I thought for a moment.

"If it gets too late, I'll call you a cab to make sure you get home," he added.

A gentle breeze caressed my face, and as I looked up at Zeke, I thought that it would be okay for me to go to his house for just a few minutes…especially if he was going to call a cab to get me home. It would save me time in the long run as I would first have to catch the subway to Center City and then take the 31 bus to my home in West Philly. Yes. A cab ride would be faster. Besides, I was tired.

Zeke's smile broadened as we began the short walk to his two-story row home. All along the way, I could hear the sounds of his neighborhood alive with activity. Cars rolled by with music ascending as they approached, diminishing as they blended into the sounds of children playing and buses rolling by leaving plumes of dark exhaust fumes in their wake. People were happy that summer was just around the corner. Two men walked past Zeke and were smoking what I thought was a cigarette. I rolled my nose up as they continued down the block as the pungent smell of marijuana assaulted my nose.

Zeke looked down at me and laughed.

"What's so funny?" I asked while glancing over my shoulder.

"You," he said as he draped his arm over my shoulder. "What? You never smelled weed before?"

"It stinks."

He laughed again.

"Boy, you got a lot to learn." He rubbed my shoulder, and that made me feel good. I felt protected, and in that moment, I was sure that he wouldn't hurt me. "You know what I think?"

"What?"

"I think that you're a hell of a man."

"What makes you say that?" I asked as we turned on to his block.

"It's just that I've been around you long enough to know a good man when I see one. You're funny, and I like being around you."

"You do?" I felt my heart leap. No one had ever said that to me before.

"Of course." He pulled me closer to him. "You don't think I do?"

"It's just that you never said that before."

"I should have before now." He grinned lightly. "I should have said that long ago. Is it okay with you that I said that?"

"Yeah." I nodded as we turned and ascended the three concrete steps it took to get to his porch.

He pulled out his key and opened up the front door.

The entire house was quiet, and initially, as I looked past the living room into the dining room, I thought we were alone.

"Zeke! That you?" I heard a female voice call from somewhere upstairs.

"Yeah!" he called back as he led me up the stairs. "What you want, Mom?"

We reached the top of the steps where he nodded his head to the small bedroom that sat squarely to my right. I went in and sat down on the edge of the bed and looked out of the window at the house across the alley. Nothing to see. Zeke closed the door behind me. I looked around the small beige-colored room. Zeke's full-sized bed dominated the room. I looked at his dresser. Nothing much to see there either except for a pair of handcuffs, a police scanner, a tiny radio, and a small portable television set.

As I sat in his room, the events of the day caught up to me, and suddenly, I wasn't just tired; I was exhausted. When he came back, I would ask him to call the cab.

I looked at the bedroom door as Zeke walked in carrying a glass.

"Here." He extended the glass to me.

I accepted the glass, looking at its contents.

"It's fruit punch. Have some and relax."

I took a healthy sip.

"I better get going, Zeke. Can you call the cab for me so that I can get home? I don't want to get in trouble."

"I already did," he said. "I called them while I was downstairs."

"Well, can I at least call my mother to let her know I'm going to be late? She always says to be home before the streetlights come on."

Zeke thought for a moment and then reached down and placed his hand on my shoulder.

"Come on." He guided me toward the bedroom door. "The phone is in the kitchen."

The stairs creaked under our weight as we made our way downstairs. I looked at the worn wallpaper on the walls, old flowers ... a weird choice for wallpaper. We crossed the living room, and I noted the furniture. It consisted of a sofa, armchair, and coffee table. The sofa and armchair were covered in plastic ... the kind that my mother had because she didn't want me or my younger brothers to sit on it. It was reserved for company. We passed through the small dining room. A huge circular wooden table dominated the room. The kitchen sat just to the right, and I immediately went in, picked up the phone, and dialed my mother's number. I listened for a moment expecting to hear it ring, and then I heard an automated message, "The number you have dialed has been changed or is no longer in service. Please check your directory and dial again."

I shook my head, put the phone down, and then redialed the number. Once again, I got the same message. My mother had changed the house number and never told me. How was I going to get in contact with her?

I looked around the room. It was fully dark now, and I had to leave, even if it meant getting home late. But I was tired…extremely tired.

"You okay?" Zeke asked from the kitchen doorway.

"My mother changed the number," I said in disbelief. "Zeke, I gotta go, or I'm gonna get in big trouble." I started toward the front door.

Zeke followed right behind me.

"Wait a minute, little man. Hold up." He placed both of his hands on my shoulders and turned me around to face him. "I already called the cab to come pick you up. They'll have you home in no time. They said that they would be here in fifteen minutes. Go upstairs and lie down. I'll wait down here for them and come and get you when they get here."

I thought for a moment once again. A cab would be faster. It wouldn't be as late when I got home. I may get in trouble for being late, but I could explain that I tried to call my mother and got the "disconnected" message, and she would be able to see that the cab driver had indeed brought me home.

"Okay." I nodded.

"Good. Go upstairs and lie down. As soon as they get here, I'll come and get you."

I didn't give it another thought. I went upstairs and into his room, closing the door behind me. I don't think that I was in there two minutes before I had fallen asleep.

I woke up to music…and something heavy on top of me. The song coming from the small radio that sat on the dresser was "Dream Merchant" by New Birth. The weight on top of me was Zeke…and whatever he was doing hurt.

"Zeke…," I started to say.

"Sshhhh," he whispered in my ear. "It's gonna be all right."

"It hurts." I tried to sit up, but Zeke outweighed me by at least ninety pounds.

"It's okay," he whispered again.

"Is the cab coming?"

"It's coming," he grunted. "They'll be here soon."

I woke up the next morning with Zeke sitting barefoot beside me. The sun was shining brilliantly, but the dread that had welled up inside my chest could not have been more real or heavy had it been a ton of bricks sitting on top of me. I got up and dressed hastily. My mother was going to kill me.

"The cab never came," he said softly. "I called them twice."

I didn't say anything. I think that he could see the panic in my face. He got up and reached for the dresser and pulled out a dollar and handed it to me.

"Take that to get you home." He wasn't smiling this time. Today, he looked more somber. "I'm sorry," he whispered to me.

"I gotta go," I said and headed out of the room, down the stairs, and was on the sidewalk in a flash.

My heart beat steadily in my chest as I made my way to the subway. There was no question that I was in serious trouble. The question was, how much? I could tell her that I tried to call her, and she had disconnected the phone number. But I had never stayed out all night before, unless of course I was with my relatives.

As I turned to my block, my heart sunk even lower than it had before. I recognized my father's car parked in front of my mother's house. This was going to be bad. She must have called him some time last night.

As I got to the house, she was standing in the doorway, glaring at me with my father standing behind her.

"I can explain—" I began.

"You can explain it to me," my father cut me off. "Get on upstairs and lie across the bed."

"But I tried to call ... Mom changed the number and—"

"Boy, get upstairs!"

Nobody asked me where I was. Maybe they were just glad that I was home safe and sound, and that I would now have to be punished for being disobedient. And as I lay across my own bed and felt the lashes of my father's belt, the only things that I could think of was that I was glad that it wasn't my mother beating me because I knew it would have been far worse, and that I could never listen to "Dream Merchant" by New Birth again.

For me, the sexual experience with Stan had been pleasurable. So in my head, I connected pleasure with the act of molestation. It made me an active participant, which also brought my silence. This is an example of the trajectory that my life changed to when I was first touched. I knew how it felt, and if the man was someone that I trusted or, even more importantly, placed strong value in our relationship, then I would be a willing participant. It is the adult that has the power, wisdom, and knowledge to keep control of a situation. Children act out. Adults guide and lead. A child, if left to his or her own devices, will seek out what feels good to his or her body and often revert to their previous history of experiences. Gay men sleep with men by nature, so it is only natural to want to experience sex with an adult because the child doesn't know that he isn't ready for this type of experience. Childhood is for believing in Santa Claus, birthday parties, school trips, spelling bees, and finding out what you like and don't like in the people that you surround yourself with. Childhood is for discovering the world under the protection of your parents and adult guardians.

Sex shouldn't happen until the child becomes a young adult. But times have changed. The very definition of childhood has changed. We live in an age where information is only a mouse click away. We have devices that keep us in touch with one another and the world. A child's innocence is cut short by the easy access of information, whether it is true or not. Zeke stayed around me until he got what he wanted, and like most predators, he waited patiently until it was time to make his move. Maybe I was one of the many young people that he had taken advantage of. Maybe he was sleeping with Dina all the while. I have no way of knowing this because for the short amount of time that I was with him, we never talked about her. We only talked about me. He made me feel special in a way that made me want to be whatever he wanted me to be. I have no doubt that he knew exactly what he was doing. Still, Zeke and I shared a friendship. It was special to me because I wanted it to be. If sex was part of that friendship, then it was okay with me.

Some people reading this will think to themselves that if this is what I wanted, then why am I upset about it now? The answer is that I'm not upset about it at all ... or at least, I'm not upset about Zeke per se. Maybe about the time he kept me out all night long, but even with that, I wasn't overtly angry with him. People that have been groomed have been altered emotionally. Up until recently, I didn't think that I was an abuse survivor. But the reality is that I am. It doesn't matter if I wanted sex from Stan, Zeke, or any other adult male. A child is not emotionally equipped to handle the consequences that come with sex. All they know is that it feels good. That's it. End of story. We don't think about the life-changing repercussions that can occur when you have sex too soon. Back in the seventies, it was sexually transmitted diseases and unwanted pregnancies ... Now sex with the wrong person too soon can give you a lifetime chronic disease or even kill you. It is more important now than ever to understand that knowledge is power, and we must be there to direct our children's lives.

When the semester ended, I left that school and moved to high school. It was in those next four years that I would find out even more about myself and then store it into my mental Rolodex for later use.

For the next two years, I didn't see Zeke or give him that much thought. But simply because I didn't see him didn't mean that the bond established had been broken. Even though I still couldn't bring myself to listen to "Dream Merchant" by New Birth, I was able to compartmentalize my interactions and subsequent thoughts of Zeke. His keeping me out all night long was a mistake, and I believed him when he said that he had made several attempts to call a cab for me that night even though I know now that no such call had ever been made. Zeke was still someone that had elicited feelings of safety in me, and it was those feelings that superseded my common sense.

I was fifteen years old when we moved to Mt. Airy from West Philadelphia, but until the move had been completed, I had to finish out the year at the high school that I loved in that part of town before starting anew at a high school located in the suburbs. The commute from Mt. Airy to West Philly was long. It entailed a long thirty-minute bus ride to the Broad Street subway, a twenty-minute ride on the subway train into Center City, and then another forty-minute bus ride out to West Philly.

The subway took me right past the stop that I used to go to the school where Mr. Jackson taught...and where I met Zeke. As I rode the train past this stop, I would often wonder how he was and if he was doing okay. And one day, I got off the train when it pulled up to the Broad and Wyoming station and walked the few blocks to Zeke's house.

Classes were winding down, and schools were preparing for the summer break. The weather was warm. As I made my way to Zeke's house, I wondered if he would remember me, and if he did, if he would be glad to see me. I didn't have any expectations as I walked down his block and approached his house. A Mister Softee ice cream truck rang its familiar chimes as it cruised slowly down his block passing by me as I ascended the steps to his house. I knocked on the door and waited patiently for someone to answer. To my surprise, he answered without me having to knock twice.

"Heyyyy." He widened the doorway. "I haven't seen you in a long time. How have you been?"

"Fine." I smiled warmly. I had no idea how happy I would be to see him after all this time.

"Come on in." He stepped aside, allowing me to pass him. "I missed you, boy."

"I missed you too. I've been busy with school. We just moved up to Mt. Airy. My mother bought a house up there, and we're just getting settled in." I looked around me. The house hadn't changed at all.

"So what are you now, a sophomore?" he asked.

"Yep. I'm going to be a junior in the fall."

"You want something to drink?" he asked while starting toward the kitchen.

"Nahh. I'm okay. I just wanted to stop by to see how you were."

"I'm glad you did." He took a step back in blue jeans and bare feet, looking at me in that disarming way.

I felt the butterflies in my stomach.

"Look at you." He brought his hand to his chin. "How old are you now?"

"Fifteen."

"You're a grown man," he said, and then he reached out and wrapped his arms around me, hugging me tightly. "It's so good to see you."

"Me too."

"Look, I was getting ready to take a shower because I have to be somewhere real soon. Can you come back again?"

"Sure." I nodded.

"Damn, it's good to see you." His face seemed to be alight with amazement.

I didn't say anything. Actually, I was a little disappointed. I was hoping that we could spend some time together. I wanted to tell him about high school and how much I had changed. But I also realized that once I saw Zeke again, all the old feelings about him came back. It seemed like nothing had changed for him in regard to me. It felt like years hadn't passed at all. I didn't want to have sex with Zeke. What I really wanted was to reestablish our friendship. Sex with Zeke was overshadowed by a dark cloud, perhaps remnants of what had happened the night that he kept me out all night long when I was thirteen. Zeke wasn't old enough to be my father, but he could certainly fill the role of an older brother. Despite what he did two years prior, in my mind, I had forgiven him because what was done was done. My relationship with Zeke was in many ways like being in love with someone who hurt you, but you continued to love them despite the pain they inflicted. Realistically, I knew that I wasn't in love with Zeke, but there was a part of me that was enamored with him.

"Can you come back tomorrow?" he asked as I turned to leave.

"Hmmmm?"

"Can you come back tomorrow? There's someone I want you to meet."

I felt my lips turn up into a smile.

"Sure." I paused in his doorway and then wrinkled my forehead in curiosity. "Who is it?"

"He's a friend of mine. Can you swing by tomorrow at the same time?"

I nodded.

"Okay." I was through the door in a flash. "I'll see you tomorrow."

The following day turned out to be an exceptionally hot day. Summer had kicked in early and was in a great mood. My classmates were already in summer mode and ready for trips to the shore. For me, I would be heading to South Carolina to stay with my grandparents for the summer. As I made my way to Zeke's house, I wondered who he wanted me to meet. I hadn't heard anything about Dina since I had gone to high school. I wondered for a moment if he wanted me to meet another girl that he was seeing but then dismissed the thought. I didn't think that Zeke would do to me what Dina had done just two years prior. When we first met, he said that I wouldn't get hurt like that again.

I knocked on the front door, waited for a moment, looking up the block. Maybe it was because of the time of day, but it was quiet with the exception of the whirring of box fans in some of the windows of the neighboring homes. The door opened, and Zeke stood before me in jeans and a T-shirt. He didn't say anything.

"Hey, Zeke," I broke the awkward silence. I thought for a moment that maybe he'd forgotten that I was coming by.

"Come on in." He widened the door for me, and I walked past him. It was hot in the living room ... so hot that I could feel the sweat trickling down the center of my back.

"Is your friend here?" I asked while heading toward the steps.

Zeke nodded. Something was missing. He was behaving a little bit differently than he had in the past. As I ascended the steps to the second floor and turned to enter the bedroom, the first thing that I noticed was that the curtains were drawn, framed around a nineteen-inch box fan that was whirring incessantly. The second thing that I noticed was the boy sitting on the edge of the bed. He was dark skinned with big brown eyes and a short Afro. We stared at each other for a moment, and then I looked back at Zeke who had just entered the room.

"This is Damon," he said while closing the bedroom door.

"Hi." I looked back at Damon who managed a small smile.

"It's hot in here," Zeke said. "Take off your shirt."

What was missing was the candor that I was used to from Zeke. I took my shirt off without question, noting that Zeke was watching my every move. The joy that he had expressed when he saw me just the day before was gone... replaced by something else. I just didn't know what the "something else" was.

"I want you to do something for me," Zeke said while removing his shirt. "Something that would mean a lot to me."

I looked at Damon. Damon looked at me, and then I turned my attention to Zeke... and then I understood. I watched Zeke as he unbuckled his jeans. Yes. I understood what he wanted me to do.

Hindsight is twenty-twenty... always. Don't let anyone tell you differently. When I look back at my actions that afternoon in that stifling hot bedroom, I wish that I could take it back. But something bigger happened to me that day. When you're fifteen, you really think that you're grown and capable of making your own decisions. You think that you are mature enough to understand what is going on around you. I didn't know at the time that Zeke needed to be in control of the situation that he put me or any other young person in... male or female. I am convinced to this day that he had sex with Dina and then cast her aside like she was nothing. He didn't do this with me because there was never an opportunity for him to do so. I realize now that Zeke could turn on the charm just as easily as someone could turn on the light to illuminate a darkened room. He was the ultimate predator. I know this now ... but I didn't know it then. That afternoon in Zeke's room, he simply watched Damon and me. His face betrayed no emotion or, at least, nothing that I could read. I didn't understand that he was manipulating Damon just as much as he was manipulating me. And this is the scary part for anyone reading this book now because in this day in age, people like Zeke have grown more depraved. They rape without thought. They imprison without thought. And yes, they even kill without thought. Damon and I were both pawns; we just didn't know it.

What had happened with Damon had only happened once. I came by to see Zeke two times after that incident. The first was just to say hi to him, regardless of whether Damon was there or not. The last time was to say goodbye. In my mind, meeting Damon had done two things. The first was that it had begun to chip at the bond that had been established with Zeke and me. There was another boy in the mix. Whatever we were didn't include a third person. The second is that I had been replaced. In two years, Zeke had found someone else ... not that I could blame him. I had disappeared without a trace, never to be heard from again for two years. It stood to reason that he had found someone new. But he was glad to see me. I didn't understand that. None of this made any sense to me.

With the sun riding high in the sky and temperatures soaring, I made my way to Zeke's house. Sweat dripped down the sides of my face as I turned to his block. I had no idea what to expect when I arrived. I didn't know if he would want me to have sex with Damon again. I didn't even know if Damon would be there. As I approached the familiar two-story house, I saw someone sitting on a broken-down chair on the concrete porch. Damon looked up at me as I stopped at the base of the steps. I noticed for the first time that he had traces of a thin mustache. He was wearing a light-blue short-sleeved T-shirt and jeans.

"Zeke ain't here," he said while standing up slowly.

I nodded my head.

"You live here now?" I asked, already knowing my answer.

"I stay here," he answered. "But I don't live here."

"What's the difference?"

"I just…stay here. But Zeke ain't here now. He at work."

"Okay." I turned to leave.

"Wait!" He perked up. "Jerry, right?"

I turned to look at him. He was reaching into his pocket and pulled out a crumpled pack of cigarettes. He lit one and then attempted to pass it to me. I shook my head.

"I don't smoke."

He chuckled, and in that moment, I saw the boyishness in Damon. He couldn't have been that much older than me. I'm guessing that he was about seventeen…maybe eighteen tops. He took a deep drag of the cigarette that he initially offered me and then hopped down to the sidewalk. He was a little taller than me, his frame lanky.

"I'll walk you to the train."

"How'd you know I took the train?"

"Zeke told me."

I shrugged as we started down the block. We walked in silence. The air was oppressive.

"How did you meet Zeke?" I asked while taking a side glance at Damon.

He exhaled a plume of light-blue cigarette smoke and then looked back at me.

"At the store he worked at." He turned his attention to the street ahead just as a garbage truck rumbled by. "I was hungry. I took some stuff and got caught. Zeke took me in."

I nodded.

"How'd you meet him?" he asked me.

"A couple of years ago. I was in the eighth grade. I met him through a girl at school."

"No shit? He was a guard at your school?"

"No. I was kinda going out with some girl in my class. She dumped me for him."

"And she introduced you two? That's fucked up."

I nodded as we walked past a grocery store.

"Yeah," I mumbled.

Damon took another deep drag of his cigarette, looking as if he was in deep thought.

"You like him?" he asked quietly. I knew that he was referring to Zeke.

"He's all right." I looked over at him. "Do you feel funny about what we did?"

He took another hit off his cigarette and then chuckled lightly while exhaling the smoke through his nose.

"No." He smiled at me. "It was fun."

"I guess." I shook my head slowly. "I guess."

"Are you coming back over today?"

"I don't think so."

"Why not?"

"I have too much stuff to do when I get home," I lied.

The truth was that I really didn't want to come back. Damon seemed like a nice-enough guy, but he lived with Zeke. There really was no reason for me to come back again. Besides, the neighborhood that I lived in was at least an hour away by train and bus. Still, I felt like I owed Zeke a formal goodbye. It just wasn't going to be done today.

"Cool," Damon said as we reached the entrance to the Broad Street subway.

"Thanks for walking me." I looked Damon.

"I'll see ya, Jerry," he said as he turned around to head back to Zeke's house.

As I descended the steps into the cool of the dark subway station, it dawned upon me that he used my name more than Zeke ever had in the entire time that I had known him.

A few weeks had gone by since my last visit to Zeke's house. Now, as the subway train pulled into the Broad and Wyoming station, I ran the speech that I had prepared to give Zeke in my head. I was scheduled to start my junior year at a Catholic high school in Wyncote. I hated the idea of changing schools and leaving all my friends behind, but I didn't have a choice in the matter. What I was about to do felt like a breakup, and for the life of me, I didn't understand why. All I knew was that it had to be done. I didn't feel right disappearing from Zeke's life again without warning. I owed him an explanation.

It was overcast that day, but the weather was still warm and muggy. I wanted to get this over with and make it as quick as possible. It took me seven minutes to get to his house. I knocked on the door and waited patiently for either Zeke or Damon to answer.

The door opened slowly, and I stood face to face with Zeke's mother. She was somewhat tall ... a little taller than me, fair skinned with small brown eyes. She had her hair pulled back and tucked neatly underneath a silk scarf. I had seen her before in passing and always thought that she was taller than what she was, certainly taller than the woman that was standing before me now.

"Hello." Her voice came out small and tight.

I had heard her calling out to Zeke from her bedroom and always assumed that she was bigger.

"Hello, Mrs. Price." I have never used Zeke's last name before. I wasn't even sure if Price was her last name.

"I remember you." Her voice had an edge to it, something that I didn't recognize in the past. "You're Zeke's friend."

I nodded.

"Yes, ma'am. Is he home?"

She pulled her yellow housecoat around her, and I could see her eyes clouding over.

"I'm sorry, young man, but Zeke is gone." She took a deep breath. "Damon done shot him to death in the house. It happened a week ago."

My mouth dropped open. I didn't even know that Zeke had kept a gun in the house.

"I heard him yell for me when I was downstairs. He said—" Her words broke off as a tear slid down her face. "I'm sorry."

I could feel my heart beating in my chest. Zeke was dead? And Damon killed him? Why?

"I'm sorry, Mrs. Price." I didn't know what else to day.

She gave me a slight smile, a smile that showed that she was trying to be brave.

"It's okay, son." Her voice came out whispery, her pain evident.

I turned to leave, not knowing what else to say. I had just talked to Damon a few weeks ago. I don't know what would have made him do it. And just like that, it was over. I had closure. It just wasn't the closure that I had in mind.

WHERE IS GOD?

I remember my mother teaching me how to pray the Lord's Prayer when I was a little boy. I couldn't have been older than four or five when she taught me how to kneel beside my bed at night before I went to sleep and pray this simple prayer. I didn't know what I was saying or why, but I knew that I was sharing a special moment with my mother.

As I got older and discovered the concept of God, I realized that there was something much bigger than me at work in the world. I remember praying to God to take away what I was feeling about men. I remember not wanting to be drawn to other boys but feeling powerless as my attractions overtook me. There were times that I felt that God heard me, and I would interact with girls the best way that I knew how. Most times, those ways weren't good enough. I didn't know then that there really was no right way to interact with girls. You simply had to be yourself and hoped that the girl liked you for you.

When you're young, your whole world is school, home, and what social life you create for yourself. I would lie awake at night, praying that something would change inside of me so that I could be like the other boys in school. I didn't have the wisdom at the time of knowing that every teenage boy goes through some type of struggle even if his world seems rosy in comparison to yours.

I've held on to my belief in God oftentimes like it was my life raft. Throughout my life, I could remember having candid conversations with God in my mind. At the time that I was interacting with

Stan, I remember not wanting anything else to come between us, not because of the sex, but for something more.

When I was with Stan, I felt protected. I had an adult male who would protect me in case things went wrong for me. I had someone to talk to about my struggles, and I knew that he would listen. And then, there was the sex. I enjoyed being with him and knew enough to keep my mouth shut about it. Stan was nothing like my biological father, both in good ways and not so good ways. I genuinely thought that I was the only one in his life. I thought that I was special because he made me feel that way. At the time, I thought that I was lucky to have a father figure in my life, and sleeping with him was just icing on the cake.

Since I wasn't telling anyone about what was happening with Stan, I was living in a bubble of sexual abuse that I wasn't even aware of. I had no way of knowing who Stan really was or that there were more victims out there besides me.

My belief in God was, is, and always will be strong and deep. I've endured pain, but I've also experienced joy. Stan only lasted for a year; Mr. Jackson and Zeke, only a few months in total … But through it all, I've managed to pray my way through it.

My belief in God got me through the worst times in my life. I've read that it is in deep-seated pain that when you cry out to God, he/she makes him/herself known. There were times in my life where I relied strictly on faith, and then conversely, there were times where faith eluded me completely.

I've heard that who I thought I was would go straight to hell. I still hear it, but now I realize that it is my love for God and God's love for me that renders that statement false. Straight Christians don't understand the harm that they do in condemning gay men and women when they repeatedly invoke the passage in Leviticus that bolsters their prejudice against the gay community. I used to believe that my loving another man would be equivalent to purchasing a one-way ticket to hell. I've been to churches that build entire sermons about that verse repeatedly. I've been in congregations where people would nod in agreement to fire-and-brimstone preaching against people of the LGBT community.

But this is what I believe:

God created me in his/her image. I've cried out to him/her, and my prayers have been heard and answered even if the answer was no. What it does not say in that verse in Leviticus is that we are going to hell. All it says is that "man shall not lie with man as he does with woman, it is an abomination." It doesn't say that if you do, you will go to hell. You can interpret that passage any way that you like. What I know is that God's love for me will supersede anything that I have done or think of doing. It doesn't matter what any pastor of any church has to say about it because if you dig deep enough, you will find something that displeases God in their past, and that sin is no bigger or worse than mine.

I've held on to God, and he/she has never abandoned me. I keep referring to God as he/she because I believe that God encompasses the wisdom of both sexes. God is both father and mother. God is protector and conqueror. God is everything, and whatever we understand about him/her is nothing compared to what God really is. There are people that will read this and think that I don't know what I am talking about, or that I have no right to say what I am saying. Since God as I know him/her has directly impacted me, that gives me the right to say anything that I want regardless of what you may believe, just like you can say what you want about God.

People that don't believe in God question his/her existence. The argument always comes back to, "If God really exists, and he is so perfect, why does he permit pain and suffering? Why do innocent people die and others that deserve death live?"

I can't answer that. I am not God. What I do know is that what happened to me was supposed to happen to me. The trajectory of who I would have been was never the person that I ultimately wound up becoming. Tragic events make you stronger in one way or another. You have to learn to live with the pain … whether the loss would be that of a loved one or your own innocence.

The man I would have been would never have been able to write this book. The man I would have been would not have experiences to draw on to put this out there for the world to see. God never left me even at the height of my abuse. At the end of the day, people have free will, and they do things based on whoever it is they are at that moment in time. A molester today may not be a molester tomorrow. A victim today may not always be a victim, but instead, choose to do something more with their lives. God never promised us that life would be perfect. God only promised that he/she would be there to get us through it.

Throughout my life, I had sought God in churches, religious institutions, and people, only to find that God had been with me all along. In my addictions, he/she has rescued me. In my deepest pain, he/she has comforted me.

When people that claim to know God speak ill of me in his/her name, that person isn't really speaking for God as much as they are using God to substantiate their own incorrectness. You cannot claim to know and love God and have hate in your heart. It's that simple. You cannot claim to be bound by the Holy Spirit and then commit heinous acts in God's name. You cannot pick and choose which parts of the Bible that you want to believe and totally disregard the others. God doesn't work like that. Never has … never will.

THE ILLUSION OF INNOCENCE

I went to high school at the age of fourteen. I had no idea what to expect, but I embraced it wholly. My mother had enrolled me into an inner-city all-boy Catholic high school. This school was different in so many ways from my elementary school and the junior high school that I had just left. The first and most obvious difference was the size. The school was huge. Because of that, there was a place for me to belong...I simply had to find it. Unlike my elementary school where I was living in a capsule surrounded by the same people year after year, I was now exposed to different people that varied from class to class.

The funny thing about all this was I remember distinctly encountering some of the boys that I had shared four years of my life with in elementary school. There were about six of them, and I could tell that the idea of high school unnerved them. When they saw me, they wanted me to join them. I guess their thinking was that there was strength in numbers, and they wanted as many people with them as they could get. What they didn't realize was that I had been on my own for so long that I didn't feel a need to belong with them. I was excited about meeting new people and didn't really want to go back to the way that things had been when we were cooped up together back at that small Catholic elementary school we had at one time shared. I guess they forgot that I had been on the outside and had resided there for so long that I really didn't need them. I didn't dismiss them as much as I just went about my business. I wanted to make new friends and find a niche that suited me. For the first time, I had the luxury of selecting my friends as opposed to my associates selecting me. For once, I had a choice. I could take my time and find my way, and I could do this without fear of rejection. And if I found myself in the unique position of being rejected, for once, I had a choice. I could make new friends. I had options, and it felt good.

What these guys felt about me, I honestly couldn't tell you. But whatever it was, it didn't matter. I began meeting people, and as my freshman year of high school moved forward, the images of my molestations slid further and further behind me. Or at least I thought it had. I began creating short stories that now included new-found friends, and it was great. My world included new friends as well as friends that I created. I wrote stories that were intriguing and sophomoric in their creation. But this was who I was, and I was enjoying it.

I was catching a glimmer of sunshine . . . seeing the potential for how life could be. As fall moved into winter and winter into spring, I found a niche of friends that I actually bonded with. These guys were my buddies, and we had one major thing in common: we wanted to make a difference in our community. John, Carl, Mike, and Edwin became my best friends, and for a short time, we were inseparable. We belonged to the same organization in high school, CSC, which stood for Community Service Corps. We teamed up with our high school affiliates that were comprised of our female counterparts at the all-girl school located a short distance from where we were, and we had a blast.

I felt like I had a chance at feeling normal . . . something that I felt evaded me for years. At this time, I never thought about what happened with Stan, or my homeroom teacher, or my uncle for that fact. I felt like things were right with the world. I continued writing, and I found to my amusement that I was good at what I did. I would fill notebooks with short stories, taking them from class to class, and in most of them, the students that sat within a close approximation to me couldn't wait to read what I had written the day before. The only thing that was missing was a girlfriend that I felt would complete me.

Now what I think is so important for everyone to know . . . especially women, is that deception was never in the forefront of my mind. I really thought that I had the capability of being in a loving relationship with a woman even if there wasn't a man in my life to show me how. I didn't think that the underlying drive to be with a man would overtake my life, and I never thought that I would deliberately ever hurt a woman.

Remember, I had no role models. My father wasn't there to show me how to love a woman honestly and openly. And even if he were, he didn't know how to show a woman how much he loved her, if he were even capable of such an emotion. He knew how to dominate women, and if he had been around, I believe that this is what he would have shown me and my younger brothers how to be.

I didn't know at this point in time how to be the man that I thought God intended me to be. There were so many components that contributed to what I wanted, but above and beyond, there were two things that stood out quite strongly in my mind. The first was being a part of the masses. What I mean by that is that I wanted to be just like everyone else. I wanted to grow up, date a few girls, and then settle down with the right one and get married. I saw this as being remotely possible, but it meant fighting the person that continually crept on me like a thief in the night. And that brings me to my second point.

How could I love a woman completely when deep down inside, something raged in me that I strongly believed was counter to what I thought I should become? This attraction that I had to the same sex could ruin me, both from a social and psychological standpoint. How could I deal with that? What could I do about it? What were my choices?

That was easy. My choices were to continue to date girls and pray that this thing inside of me would go away and become the man that I should be *or* succumb to it and be an outcast. This was a no-brainer. Being an outcast was not an option because as I stated previously, the emotion that had been blown out of proportion for me was acceptance. Years had gone by with me existing on the outskirts of my classmates. I wanted to belong. I felt like it was within my grasp because I was in an environment where I could do that.

During the summer of my freshman year of high school, I found a summer job, which would teach me more about myself at that time than I ever thought possible. It was through a local organization that I landed a job as a package delivery boy at Children's Hospital of Philadelphia. I worked in the mailroom with several adult men who were as far from gay as my father. I liked them, but in retrospect, even they knew that something was wrong with me. Although they never came out and deliberately said it, they questioned my sexuality because I didn't act like a typical boy. I didn't talk about the girls I dated because there weren't any to talk about. These men talked about women all the time, and at that point, I wanted to be like them. I couldn't put the feeling to rest.

It was around this time that I met a young girl named Cherry. She also worked for the summer in the hospital. I couldn't tell you what department she worked in, but she was sweet and kind to a fault. She was a big girl...big boned, big hips, large breasts, skin the color of mahogany with Hershey-chocolate-colored eyes. When I think back on it, I believe that it was me that made the first move and began talking to her, and we hit it off right away.

One of our favorite pastimes was going into Center City when we got paid and going to the arcade to play the pinball machines and then going to the movies. We would catch the matinee at the local theater watching all the horror movies that had just hit the scene. And for a while, all was right with the world. I honestly didn't know what to do with Cherry outside of just hanging out with her. I know what guys my age said what they did with girls, but that didn't feel normal to me. I may have had experience in having sex with another guy, but I was clearly a virgin when it came down to sex with a girl. Still, something in my mind screamed that I wanted to be normal and belong. I wanted to feel normal, and above all, I wanted to stop the record that kept playing over and over in my mind that I wasn't like all the other guys. As my relationship with Cherry progressed, and I became more and more involved with the Community Services Corps in my sophomore year of high school, normality seemed to be just within my grasp.

CSC played a vital role in forming the good in me because the organization itself did so much good within the community. As a cohesive unit, we would go to orphanages and play with the kids that were there. Those children would call us "mommy" and "daddy" because they didn't have anyone that they could look up to. In retrospect, those children were just as lost as I was. We would go to convalescent homes and sing songs with the elderly ... some of which were placed there and then forgotten by their families.

We went on "leadership weekends," which was another way for me to feel as if my life was going in the right direction. On these weekends, we would go to a camp and run through exercises designed to instill leadership qualities in each of us, building up teamwork and camaraderie, as well as learn about the goodness of God.

At Christmastime, we would volunteer for a program called Operation Santa Claus, where we would go to gift-wrapping parties at one of the local area parishes. We would prepare gifts for needy families in the area by sorting the toys and gifts donated to meet the age requirements of the children of the households, and then on Christmas Eve, we would dress up like Santa Claus and his helpers and distribute them.

The expressions on the faces of the children when we walked through the door were priceless. They truly thought that we were Santa Claus and had come to drop off their toys. After this was done, we would go to the Sheraton Hotel in Center City for a massive midnight mass. This was what I thought Christmas was all about.

At this point in time, I was surrounded by other teenagers just like myself who strived to do well in our respective communities. Looking back on this time in my life, I felt like this was a time of innocence. I could immerse myself in the good that was expected of me and, for once, live up to those expectations. I could forget about the past and concentrate on the future. It was also around this time that my interest in writing took off. I realized that I had a gift. Writing became a gift that was solely mine, and I belonged with a group of people that wanted me. My friends, John, Carl, Mike, and Edwin were amazing ... not because they were extraordinary, but because they allowed me to be included in their inner circle. I never wanted to sleep with any of these guys. They were simply wonderful friends that made life normal for me. And indeed, everything was as normal as could be until my family moved to Mt. Airy, and I had to leave this school for another.

❧❂❧

Some women reading this book will say things like, "Well, I can't feel sorry for you because you knew you were gay, and you still got involved with girls! Why would you do such a thing?"

And to that, I would have to respond and say, you're absolutely correct. Part of me knew that I was gay, and another part of me … the greater part of me wanted to be normal. After all, who would want to live on the outskirts of society? Who in their right mind would choose being gay over being straight? There were no role models for gay people in the seventies. There were no communities that could uplift me. I felt like I was all alone with these feelings that I didn't understand. And when you're all alone, you think that you have to conform to the way that society is and wants you to be in order for you to fit in. Keep in mind that the emotion that was thrown out of whack for me was the need to be accepted, and my problem was exacerbated tenfold.

Deception was never part of my intention. It was simply the way that I thought things should be. I had teachers, friends, family, and psychiatrists telling me so. Naturally, I thought that if I just found the right girl, I would be okay. At the time, I didn't know that there was a community of men that felt like I did on the inside. The only thing that I wanted was to be happy, and being happy meant that I had to belong. And as I grew into young adulthood, I thought that maybe it was possible to find what I was looking for all along. My freshman and sophomore years in high school were perhaps my best years. But tougher years were coming.

MT. AIRY

In 1977, we moved from West Philadelphia to Mt. Airy. At that time, Mt. Airy was still somewhat affluent, playing home to a mixture of black, white, and Hispanic residents. My mother had purchased a three-bedroom row home, and I was happy. The neighborhood was clean, but it also meant I had to change to another high school, which was something I didn't want to do. I didn't want to leave my friends. I didn't want the leadership weekends to stop. Most of all, I didn't want to meet anyone new. I had found order in my life, and I didn't want it to change.

My mother had taken me to a new high school on the outskirts of our neighborhood, and I didn't like it. Maybe it was because I didn't want to leave my old inner-city high school. Maybe it was because I didn't want to leave my friends. Or maybe I didn't want to start all over again. All of it didn't matter. The bottom line was I was leaving a place where I was included and accepted, going into an uncertain environment.

As I became acclimated to my new surroundings, my relationship with Cherry was starting to change. Mt. Airy was a long way from West Philadelphia. As a matter of fact, it would take me a bus ride, a train ride, and then a trolley ride to get to her. She had invited me to go to Hershey Park, but to make this trip, it required the family to be up and ready by 5:00 AM. Since it already took me two hours to get to her house, it was agreed that in order for me to make this trip, I would come and spend the night at her house.

I slept on the sofa while her parents slept upstairs and she in her own room. Sometime that evening, she crept downstairs in a light-blue gown, and I was awakened by her kissing me gently on the mouth. She had seated herself on the floor beside me and rested her head on my chest, and immediately, I felt the stirrings of a teenage boy. I imagine she could feel my heart beating in my chest because I realized what was getting ready to happen. As my mind began to whirl, I pulled her to me and laid her down on the couch. We began to kiss and touch one another until I found myself inside of her. She murmured something in my ear, but held me tightly, and thinking back on it, I realized that what she said was that it hurt. But I didn't stop. I couldn't even if I wanted to. She kissed me, held my shoulders, and then wrapped her arms and legs around me, and I remember thinking, "This is what all the guys were talking about! My god, this feels amazing!" I also knew that I didn't want to get her pregnant, so just before passion took over me, I pulled myself out of her. I didn't realize that at that point, it wouldn't have mattered whether I did that or not, if she were going to become pregnant, she would have, just by my being inside of her as I had been leaking seminal fluid the entire time. I had lost my virginity to a girl one year my senior and thought that this would replace all the feelings that I had bubbling inside of me. As wonderful as it felt, all it did was add another layer to my confused state. Now I was hungry for men and women. I didn't know what to call myself. I didn't even know if there was a name for me. Being with Cherry didn't make me any more normal than I had been before her. And after our outing at Hershey Park, I knew that I would have to break it off with her. I was in a different high school that was filled with different experiences. And along with those experiences would come different girls until I would meet my first great female love.

The new high school was smaller...maybe a quarter of the size of my inner-city high school. The entire black population of that school could fit in two SEPTA buses. And as a matter of fact, there was an actual bus that transported the majority of the African American students to the high school. The bus was nicknamed "the Soul Train"

by one of the teachers. There was an undertone of racism that ran through the school much like an undercurrent beneath the surface of a seemingly calm riverbed. Occasionally, it would rear its ugly head in the harsh comments made by some of the students... students whose parents simply hadn't taught them any better.

I was caught in the middle. I had no sense of belonging, which made me hate the school even more. The African American population was so different from the body of students that I had been used to associating with, that I didn't know how to interact with them. In many ways, I felt isolated. I felt like I wasn't black enough to be with the black students, and I wasn't white. I sought comfort in my writings, creating an imaginary world of circumstances where I not only belonged, but where my personality was allowed to flourish.

I did manage to make a few friends, and I latched on to them like a drowning man clinging to a life raft. One of my friends would become my best friend, and then later, my steady girlfriend. This wouldn't happen until 1978.

Disco had burst to the scene with a driving, repetitious beat. Donna Summer was the reigning queen, releasing hit after hit of dance tunes that seemed to go on forever, and I was enraptured. WCAU 98.1 FM rocked the airwaves with the disco beat, and I learned how to hustle, complete with death drop dips and lifts. Deney Terrio hosted *Dance Fever*, which broadcast on channel 10, and my best friend and I began dancing together. Trina Bailey was something else. She was two years my junior, beautiful, a little chubby, and deliciously full figured. She was shorter than me, and nearly everyone thought that we were dating before we actually crossed that line.

I made her the center of my world, and she made me the center of hers. It was a match made in heaven, at least for the time being. We started off as friends and wound up being something entirely different, but the funny thing about being with her was that it felt natural. Being with Trina was almost as natural as being with a guy. And in the back of my head, I remember thinking that if I had to be with a woman, then let it be her. She had this way about her that was enthralling. When I talked, she listened, and vice versa; when she spoke, I listened to her. We spent almost every waking moment together, and when we weren't together, we were on the phone.

I had dated girls before Trina, but out of all of them, she was the only one that I could really honestly say that I was in love with ... or at least in love as a teenage boy could be with a girl. I didn't have anyone to teach me how to love, and I believe that if my father had been in my life, he wouldn't have been able to lead me the way I needed to be led. After all, my father was a womanizer. Had he been present in the lives of my brothers and me, he would have taught us how to be the same way. I was confused enough without adding being a womanizer to my résumé. I knew that he and his brothers had a history of abusing their women, some of which I witnessed personally.

He would have brought out the worst in me when it came to dealing with girls. But I believe with everything within me that he would not have been able to influence my behavior when it came to Trina.

Hindsight is twenty/twenty. You'll hear me say this repeatedly throughout this work. If I had the chance to do it all over again, I would have made different choices. I had selected my very first girlfriend because I heard that this was what you were supposed to do. I wasn't a good boyfriend to her not because of my homosexuality but because I was looking for a prettier girl. In my mind, I thought that I was supposed to be with a girl that looked like Thelma from the hit show *Good Times*, yet I didn't know how to interact with girls. There was nobody around to tell me. At the same time, I wasn't the guy that was the first choice on a girl's list. I wasn't into fancy clothes or sports. All I had was my writings, and I knew how to dance. When I think about it, I realize that I was always socially awkward. At the time, I didn't feel like it, but I see it now. In the seventies, dating girls was more like wearing a badge of honor; the prettier the girl, the higher the badge.

On the opposite end of the spectrum was being gay. That was perhaps the worst thing that you could be. I knew this as did every boy growing up in that era.

Loving Trina was easy. She had become my best friend in every way. During the summer, we were together from morning until night, and when we weren't together, we were on the phone. Consequently, I realized that the main difference between Trina and all the girls that I had dated previously is that when I was with them, I was playing a part, acting like what I thought I was supposed to act like. With Trina, there was no acting. We had become friends first. As a matter of fact, she had become my best friend. We shared so much between us that I soon realized that people were looking at us as a bona fide couple before we even acknowledged the fact that we were. During the course of our friendship and before we became an item, a boy came into my life who would remind me of who I really was. He would remind me that I had the capacity to love someone of the same sex, even if I wasn't ready for it. He would remind me that if society were more accepting, I could live a normal life loving who I wanted to love instead of loving who society said that I should be with. And yet at the time, meeting someone different would remind me that the capacity was there.

JASON

My junior year in high school was a bag of mixed emotions. I missed the inner city high school that I had spent what had, up until that point, been the happiest times of my life. I missed my group of friends. I missed the leadership weekends. I missed the organization that I belonged to called CSC.

At my new high school, I had a new best friend named Trina and a smattering of friends... or at least it felt like a smattering of friends. I never felt like I belonged. Sure, the neighborhood where I lived was nicer, but I needed to feel like I belonged somewhere. High school wasn't it. Instead, it was filled with people that I couldn't bond with no matter how I tried. It was a semilonely experience, and I fought with my mother to get back to the high school in West Philadelphia that I had left behind. She wanted me to have friends in my own neighborhood. It wasn't until later that I found out that she was worried about my commute from Mt. Airy to West Philadelphia. She was worried about the gangs that would draft young boys to join them even if they have to beat them senseless to do it.

At my new high school, they had a day to celebrate the school and the students that attended. On that day, we didn't have to wear our school uniforms or attend classes. On this spring day, the school had transformed the grounds into a carnival, complete with multiple booths, raffles, and a talent show.

I remember being alone that day, wandering from booth to booth, not necessarily being interested in anything. I remember going inside to watch the talent show, and I saw a boy sitting by himself. He was blond haired, blue eyes... and lonely. I sat beside him and started talking to him. He seemed as excited to talk to me as I was to talk to him, and we hung out for the rest of the day. He told me that his name was Jason, and at the time, I remembered not feeling anything sexual about him. Instead, I felt like I had found someone who was just as lonely as I was. But the funny thing about loneliness is that once you bring two people or more together, there is no room for loneliness. We spent the rest of the day going from booth to booth and rewatching the talent show; only now, we were viewing the festivities through a different lens. We were looking at it through the beginnings of a friendship. And honestly, friendship was all that I wanted from him at that moment. Sex never entered my mind.

We hung out the entire day, and after school was over, we walked to his home. Conversation with Jason was easy. I found out that he lived in a home for boys, and that even though he should have had more friends, I began to realize that he didn't have any. In many ways, he was just like me. We were both isolated with limited friends. We both lacked what would be considered basic social skills. What I mean by that is that we were both in some way, shape, or form, friendless, looking at our social circumstances from the outside because we didn't know how to exist on the inside. This may explain why it was so easy for us to gravitate to one another.

Ironically, I never asked him what brought him to the place where he lived. I am purposefully avoiding naming the home that he resided in for various reasons … None of them that I care to go into right now.

The important thing was that for the moment, I had found someone that I could pal around with and feel that sense of normalcy. Having one good friend for me was better than having seven or eight associates. At that time, even with the idea of sex never being too far from the center of my mind, it was the social interactions that I wanted. I wanted to belong. And yet, from day to day, being in this suburban high school only exacerbated the fact that I didn't belong at all.

To the black students, I wasn't black enough, and to the white students, I wasn't white at all. This school was such a departure from the inner-city school that I had come from that I struggled to figure out ways to either make me belong or get back to what I missed for so long.

Jason helped me forget that I didn't belong, even if it were for a few moments. Like I said, our common bond was the void that we seemed to fill in each other's lives. As we walked back to his home, I remember thinking that I had finally found a good friend. Maybe I didn't need to get back to my West Philadelphia high school after all. Maybe it was possible for me to ride out this year and the next, graduating into whatever the world had to offer me. Still, it wouldn't be long before old urges would return, and with that, issues that would change my relationship with Jason forever.

❧✖❧

I don't remember when my feelings changed about Jason. I'm willing to say that it wasn't too long after we began hanging out. We spent a tremendous amount of time together, riding our ten-speed bikes, hanging out at the mall (yes, malls did exist in the '70s), and going to and from each other's homes. Jason lived in the deep suburbs right outside of Philadelphia. My neighborhood was right on the edge of the main avenue that divided the counties. One evening, after spending the day with Jason, he walked me up this long dark road that led to the main avenue that divided the counties. This road had no streetlights and was surrounded by a dark forest on one side and an immense graveyard on the other. I don't remember what we talked about during that walk, but I sensed that something was different with us. Something was happening that both unnerved me and excited me at the same time. I remember walking in silence, just enjoying his company. Have you ever been around someone, and you didn't have to say anything at all because you knew that you were joined in some kind of way, but you just couldn't put your finger on it? That's how it was with us on that walk. When we got to the end of that long dark road, we both stopped, and he turned to face me.

"I gotta be heading back," he said softly while looking down at the ground.

"I know." And I could feel my heart steadily beating inside of my chest.

"Will you come by tomorrow?" He looked at me in the eye.

"Yeah. Sure." And without hesitation, I reached for him, pulling him to me in a tight hug. "See you tomorrow, buddy."

"Looking forward to it," he whispered while hugging me back, and then he turned his face to mine and kissed me lightly on the cheek.

He let go of me quickly with the slightest hint of a smile on his lips.

"See you tomorrow," he said while starting down the dark road.

I shook my head, not believing what had just happened. Something as simple as a kiss on the cheek unleashed a torrent of feelings that I didn't know I had. And as I walked home, I kept thinking that this was impossible. I couldn't begin to have feelings for my friend. This could mess things up for us. I couldn't be gay. That would make me all the awful things that I had been called in the past. What if someone found out? And not that this made much of a difference, but Jason was white. What would happen to us at school?

Still, I had this rush of euphoria that I couldn't share with any-one, not even Trina. You see, Trina was still one of my best friends, but I couldn't tell her about this. At the time, I didn't understand my feelings, so how could I expect her to? Instead, I went home, made myself a sandwich, and crawled into bed, thinking of tonight and trying to decipher what it all meant, if indeed it meant anything at all. I couldn't be sure, and I wanted more than anything to be sure. There was only one way that I could do this, and so by the light of a single lamp that sat on the nightstand beside my bed, I pulled out a sheet of paper and began to write a letter.

❧

I think that I dreamed of Jason that night. I'm not sure. If you can remember back to your years in high school, can you remember any-one—male or female, that you've been so infatuated with that you could actually see their face in your sleep? Well, that's what it was like for me when I woke up the next morning. I could feel Jason's lips on my cheek. I could feel his body in my arms. And most of all, I remembered the look in his eyes as he walked away from me and headed home.

You're probably asking yourself what this has to do with child molestation and its aftermath. The answer is that I had latched on to this boy, not because he presented an opportunity for me to find out something about myself that I wasn't altogether sure that I wanted to know. That would have been too easy. That's like trying to summarize the concept of the universe into one sentence. Jason represented a friend who scared the hell out of me. Yet somehow through that fear, I was able to see something in him even if I wasn't quite sure of what I was seeing. In my mind's eye, I could see possibilities even if I didn't know what possibilities there were to be had. He could be a friend that I could perhaps be myself with … the self that I didn't want to acknowledge because I didn't want to have to experience the repercussions of rejections. You see, the simple truth of the matter was deep down inside, I knew that he was just like me.

I wasn't sure about this at first. I've always been guilty of over-thinking things, and this situation was no exception. My sense of belonging was critical to my emotional well-being, and although I hated the high school that I was going to, I did have a friend that I could explore who I was as well as what I would ultimately become. I always knew that I had feelings about boys, but I wouldn't allow myself to admit it because to do so would make me the very thing that would make me the target of ostracism. I needed to belong even if my social circles were limited. The one thing that I didn't want to be was alone. As I look back on this part of my life, I realize that my sense of belonging was blown out of proportion for me. I would do any and every thing to be included … and if I wasn't, then I would be thrown into the emotional equivalent of a black hole with no way of escaping.

As I made my way to school, I kept feeling the letter in my pocket that I had written to Jason. I wondered what he would say to me after he read it. I knew that it would either make or break our friendship, and I was banking everything on a single kiss on the cheek. I pulled the letter out of my pocket and read it over again. I was careful in my language, telling him how much I cared about him but stopping short of saying that I was in love with him. And truth be told, I wasn't sure I was in love with him because at sixteen, I didn't even know what love was. Still, if he was smart, he would read in between the lines and understand what I was trying to say even if I wasn't 100 percent sure myself. I didn't have a girlfriend at the time and no prospects on the horizon. This was good because I knew that I couldn't divide my time between Jason and a girl that would ultimately want to spend all her free time with me. Or at least this is what I understood a relationship between a boy and girl to be at the time.

I must have reread the two-page letter three times before deciding that it was okay to give it to Jason. And now that I was standing in his bedroom with the door closed, with my hands shoved deeply in my pockets, I realized that the moment had arrived. He was half sitting/half lying on the edge of his twin bed, and we had just finished playing a card game called crazy eights. It's funny how I don't even remember how to play that game now, but back then, it was one of my favorite card games to play.

"I . . ." All of a sudden, my mouth felt like it was full of sand. "I have something for you."

I shifted my weight from one foot to the other as he sat upright, looking at me with a soft intensity that unnerved me all over again. I had to look away from him, catching a glimpse of my Afro in the mirror across the room.

"What is it?" he asked.

"It's a note." I swallowed. "I wrote this last night. I mean . . . you know that you're my best friend, right?"

He nodded.

"So give me the note," he said with a slight smile while extending his hand to me.

I pulled the note out of my pocket and handed it to him. The room was quiet, very quiet. It almost reminded me of how quiet it was when I was with Stan three years ago. I watched Jason as he unfolded the pieces of paper and began reading.

I remember thinking to myself that he was going to ask me to leave the house and never come back. I thought that somehow he would read in between the lines, and that what I had thought the kiss on the cheek meant was really nothing at all. I watched him intently as he continued to read the letter.

I found myself looking out the window into the forest that grew behind the building that he called home. I swallowed, tasting nothing, and as if I was acting out a scene rehearsed many times in my mind's eye before, I started toward the chair that sat in front of a small wooden desk. My jacket was hanging on the back. But just as I began to reach for it, I heard him put my note down on the bed, and he stood up.

"I feel the same way about you," he said in a voice so low that I almost didn't hear him.

He approached me, looking at me directly in the eye. "I probably feel double what you wrote."

And then he hugged me tight, and I hugged him back. I felt his lips on my cheek, and then without a moment's hesitation, he turned my face to his and kissed me full on the mouth... and I let him. I could feel my knees grow weak, and I wondered if this was what it was supposed to feel like. Was everything that I thought coming down to this one unbelievable moment?

After Jason kissed me, he took a step back and looked at me with an expression that I couldn't make out at first.

"I wished that you had said this sooner," he said. "I knew I felt like this a long time ago."

"We haven't known each other that long," I said to him as I watched his hands move toward my belt line.

"We've known each other long enough," he said, and he unbuckled my belt, allowing my pants to slide down my thighs and pool around my ankles. He pulled off his shirt, and I did the same all the while watching him, and when we finally stood naked in front of one another, I realized that looking at him was like looking at a white version of me.

He placed his hands on my chest, pushing me to the bed, and as his body settled over mine, he murmured something that I had never heard a boy say to me before. He kissed me again and murmured, "I love you."

There's a song that was released in the seventies called "A Thin Line Between Love and Hate." I believe that wholeheartedly. I also believe that there is a thinner line between love and infatuation. Looking back at the age of sixteen, I am certain that the lines between infatuation and true love were blurred, and to this day, I don't know what I was with Jason. But at that moment, I felt like I truly loved him. I say "felt" because I had never felt this way about another guy before. This had to be love.

But for as much as I may have felt about Jason, there were so many reasons why I couldn't love him. For starters, he was the same sex as me. Even though it felt great to be with him, I knew logically that there could be no future with him. At that time, I wasn't aware of any gay communities or social groups. Being gay was still a dirty word, something that you couldn't be proud of remotely, and at the time, who were the gay role models out there? Billy Crystal who played the character Jody from the series *Soap*? Elton John? No. None at all. To make matters worse, there was me being black. If you were gay, or even suspected of being gay, you were regarded as being less than a man.

You would be the target of derision and exclusion, both of which I couldn't afford as I realize now that I didn't have it in me to not care about what people thought. I believe that as a result of my molestation, the emotion thrown out of whack for me was that sense of belonging or inclusion. Being gay didn't fit into that equation.

But sleeping with Jason the few times that I did was incredible. Looking at the differences between our skins as we sweated it out between his sheets was amazing. I wanted it to last as long as possible but knew that we were living on borrowed time. For a while, things were fine. I came by, spent a little bit of time with him, and sometimes we had sex. It wasn't until Jason wanted to take things to another level that the reality of what we were doing kicked in for me.

As I stated earlier, Jason lived in a home for boys. I don't know how many boys lived in this home, but my guess would have to be somewhere between twenty and thirty. There were no women there at all … only Christian brothers. At least I don't remember seeing any women there. The other piece of the equation was that some of these boys attended the same school that Jason and I went to. Some of these boys even attended the same classes as I did. And just as I suspected, the rumors of the relationship between Jason and me began to swirl like storm clouds over a sleepy Midwestern town.

At the same time that the rumors began, Jason wanted to spend more time with me. He started talking about spending the weekends together. He spoke of sleeping in late on Saturday mornings and going to the movies after biking all day, and then coming back to his room and diving underneath the blankets again. And that's when I started pulling away from him. It started initially by my not being available to hang out after school. If he came by my house, I wouldn't be home. If he called me, I wouldn't answer, or if I did, I kept the conversation short and brief. After a while, he got the hint, and I didn't hear from him. A few weeks passed, and the rumors began to die down.

I was missing my friend. I thought that it would be safe for me to get on my bike and ride over to his house. I rode there, hoping to see him and to spend some time with him. I didn't go over there with the intention of sleeping with him. I simply wanted to see him. When I got there, I entered the house, went downstairs to the recreation room, and watched as he played pool with another black male. He looked up at me for just a second, not saying a word and then went back to his game.

I was crushed. I had been replaced. I was replaced by another boy just as quickly as Zeke had replaced me with Damon. And yet I wasn't mature enough to accept the reason why I was replaced. I'm sure that he felt as rejected by me as I did by him. But I was in his home now, and I was at an emotional loss. I didn't know what to do. I watched him play pool with his new friend for a few moments, hoping that maybe he would stop and at least acknowledge that I was there. When I realized that this wasn't going to happen, I turned and walked out of the room, but instead of leaving the house, I descended the few steps from the recreation room to a part of the house that I had never been in before. I knew that this area was where the group of boys only known to me as "the seniors" was housed. I assumed that their title was associated with their place in high school, or it could have been that they were the oldest of the boys that resided at this home. It didn't matter to me.

I started down the hallway that led to their area and was first struck by how dark it was. The hallway was lined with rooms that ran the full length of the corridor on either side. Some of the doors were partially open, but no one occupied them … at least as far as I could see. I turned to leave and started back toward the recreation room, not sure if I should say goodbye to Jason or not. As I emerged from the hallway, I was met by one of the Christian brothers who asked me why I was in this section of the house. I didn't have an answer for him. How could I? What was I going to say? I was here to see a friend of mine and found out that I was replaced by another boy? He told me that this area was off limits, and that I had no right being there. I couldn't understand why he was so angry, and at that moment, I didn't care. I think that I mumbled some type of an apology and left. But there were two things that I remember about that day. The first was that my friendship with Jason was over, and second, I knew that I was no longer welcomed in that home.

TRINA

I never told anyone about what had happened that day, nor did I tell anyone about Jason who I now realize was my first dose of infatuation. I know that he felt like love at the time, but in reality, what we were was nothing more than school-aged boys who messed around. I think that at the time we needed each other in a way that would never last long term, but would open the door for feelings and emotions to be had later on in life when we were ready for them to occur. I didn't forget Jason as much as I just put him out of my mind. It was easy because I kept thinking of the alternative. If I had continued to see him, ultimately, something would have happened to cause us to be found out. There wasn't a place for guys like us. School would have turned into something unbearable. We would have been ostracized, and I couldn't afford to let that happen. What I wanted was a normal life. I wanted to settle down into a life where things just made sense. Being with another guy, white or black, didn't make sense and didn't have a place in the world as I knew it.

I settled into normality as best as I could, while still feeling like I was on the outskirts of my own world. Trina had always been part of my world, but she would soon play a bigger role than we both could imagine. Trina was a full-figured girl with short hair, big brown eyes, and a baby face. I don't remember exactly when we started dancing together, but when we did, our friendship grew, and before I knew it, we were suddenly joined at the hip. We watched dance shows like *American Band Stand*, *Steel Pier*, and *Dance Fever* and incorporated the moves of some of the dances that we saw into our own routine. We were good, quite good actually. I focused my attention on dancing because it was the one thing that I felt good at. In many ways, it was my "go-to." It became my safe spot.

Sports had never been my thing, so there was no chance of me joining the basketball or football team. I had no desire to participate in the high school drama guild because there were no friends that I could bond with. But with dancing and having Trina by my side, I was a force to be reckoned with. We were good, and we knew it. All of a sudden, people noticed me. I wasn't a shadow on the wall anymore. But that attention came with a price. Along with the admiration came the envy, and with that envy came the inflictions of malice that some teenagers are known for. No one really knew what was going on inside me. They didn't know about the conflict that battled daily for my attention. No one knew that I was struggling to fit in. By the same token, if anyone did know, I believe that they couldn't have cared less because every teen at some point in time goes through their own personal issues. As a result, thinking of someone else's pain would probably be inconsequential.

As I think about my last two years of high school, it occurred to me that the only thing I never had the coping mechanisms to deal with was being uprooted from a high school that I loved, to being transplanted to a high school that I hated. I didn't have the social skills needed to deal with going to a school that was so different than the one that I had come from. My need to fit in was blown out of proportion that grasping to any form of reality in any way, shape, or form would have been my only recourse. It was in this that I grasped and held firmly on to Trina.

Trina had been my friend first and dance partner second. She had become so entrenched in my family that most of the family members that knew us thought that we were perfectly matched. You rarely saw one without the other. How we became so intertwined is something that I can't readily explain. What I will say is that she started off as being a good friend, and then later became something more.

The "more" started on an afternoon when we had decided to go to the movies. It wasn't a date per se, as much as it was two friends going to the movies to hang out. This was something that we did many, many times before, but on this particular day, she had changed her appearance enough that I looked at her differently.

She had purchased a ponytail and attached it to her own hair. She had put on a little makeup, a peach-colored blouse, and a brown-and-tan skirt. Trina had transformed herself into a young woman, not that I hadn't known that she was a woman all along, but this was the first time that I had truly noticed how stunning she was. I was seeing her through a new lens. She was beautiful, she was my friend, and most importantly, she was with me. And as we made our way to the theater, I couldn't help but feel the lightness in my step.

I wanted to feel like I had a place in society that was rightfully mine. I was able to put Jason out of my mind and focus on living a normal life with Trina. With Trina, everything felt right. She was beautiful, and I didn't have to act with her. There was no need to pretend with Trina because from that day at the movie theater, our relationship progressed naturally from friends to boyfriend and girl-friend. As we watched *American Hot Wax* and *American Graffiti*, I realized that love and all the wonderful things that came with it were within my grasp. With that first kiss, we missed the entire movie of *American Hot Wax*. And I remember walking her to the bus stop as a light snow began to fall, and as we watched bus after bus roll by, we kissed, and the only thing that mattered to me was her.

❧

I don't know about other gay men, but in my case, Trina was truly my best friend. Our relationship had started from friendship and blossomed into love, much to the dismay of her mother. Trina's mother didn't like me, and in retrospect, if I were her, I probably wouldn't have liked me either. Mothers can tell things about teenagers that come into the lives of their children. Perhaps she could see that I was gay, and that the only thing that I would bring her daughter was pain. It didn't matter what I felt at the time for Trina or how real those feelings were to me. I knew early on that Trina's mother and I would never hit it off.

This didn't stop us from being together, and it certainly didn't stop us from dancing. And dance we did. Our lives became a whirl-wind of emotions coupled with lots of talks about life. I still couldn't tell her about how I felt about guys. This was funny to me because I thought that I could tell her everything. And yet, looking back, I realized that I couldn't. She was my world just as much as I was hers. I felt like I belonged with and to her as much as she felt like she belonged with and to me. She had become so entrenched in my family that everyone, including myself, thought that we would ulti-mately get married.

This was not an issue of being on the "down low." I had no idea what being on the "down low" was, much less what it meant. I had pushed Jason out of my mind successfully, almost as if he didn't exist, and while I never forgot about him, he wasn't on my mind when Trina and I took our friendship into love and intimacy. I didn't see Jason in school, and to this day, I don't know what became of him.

At that point in time, it didn't matter because in my mind, I belonged to someone. I loved Trina, and it wasn't because it was politically correct for me to do so. It was because she had become my world at the time. She had this innocent way of believing in me. She saw my penchant for writing and believed that I had what it took to become an author. She was attracted to me... genuinely attracted to me. She thought that I was handsome, if not downright desirable.

I had never felt desired by a woman before... or at least up until this point in my life. I never felt like I was one of the boys that pretty girls wanted to be with. How much of this has to do with my molestation, I have no idea. Maybe I will figure it out when I com-plete this book. After all, lack of self-esteem plays a huge role with victims. Maybe we don't realize it because we are too busy living our lives respectively and accept lack of self-esteem as being our norm.

And this brings me back to Trina. Falling in love with her was easy because we already had friendship in place. Being with her inti-mately was even easier because we were already joined at the hip. Our friendship had blossomed into physical love easily. Making love with her had been nothing short of amazing... and at sixteen, I found myself doing things with a girl that I never dreamed possible. Now mind you, I still had the selfishness of a teenage boy. I knew nothing about pleasing a girl at that point. I knew where things were supposed to go, and I knew how to touch her. In my mind, it was about being gentle and savoring the moment with her. It was about becoming so enveloped in the softness and warmth of her that all time seemed to stop. It was about listening to her murmur and coo my name while she held tightly to me, and knowing in all of this that she loved me.

She understood me. She knew my body, and I knew hers … but none of this was because I had to; it was because I wanted to. With Trina, I didn't have to prove anything. She accepted me and all my idiosyncrasies. Does that mean that our relationship was perfect? No. Not by a long shot. Trina had a temper. If I did something that pissed her off, she let me know it. Sometimes I did the right thing by addressing the issue immediately, and sometimes I didn't. I didn't realize it at the time, but we were living on borrowed time. Our seemingly perfect little world would come to an end in less than a year, and once again, I would find that my life would be changing.

COMING OUT

Trina and I had become accustomed to finding dance clubs that played good music. It was the spring of '79, and disco music had reached its peak. Trina and I would catch the bus to Center City and walk around looking for a club to dance in. The Internet didn't exist back then, so the option to go online and look for a local dance club didn't exist. It was a lot more fun to go in search of a place where we could dance the night away. Sometimes we'd find it, and sometimes we didn't. The thrill was in the search, and through it all, we still had each other, so at the end of the day, it didn't matter what we found or what we didn't. But on this particular day, we were in Center City walking down Spruce Street heading toward Delaware Avenue, which ran the length of the Delaware River that separated Philadelphia from New Jersey. As we neared Broad Street, we heard music coming from the inside of a three-story building. The beat was driving, pulsating in such a way that it pulled us in immediately.

Once inside, the sounds of Gloria Gaynor, Donna Summer, The Trammps, and Chic enveloped us amid flashing strobe lights and disco balls. We danced until 2:00 AM, having the time of our lives. I never noticed that Trina was the only woman in the place. This was my introduction to my first gay bar. The bar was the Allegro, and that night would signify the changing of my life permanently. Of course, we decided to go back the following week, not realizing that we were too young to be inside of such an establishment. They carded us instantly, and that night, we didn't get to relive the events of the week before. In our minds, we had found a place where we could dance and have a good time. I wasn't interested in drinking to the excess or meeting anyone. I was only interested in dancing and getting recognized for my moves with the girl that I loved. And I got noticed... just not in the way that I initially planned.

Trina and I had gone back to the club a few times, sometimes with success, most times not. I remember noticing for the first time that the Allegro was a gay club when I took a pause from dancing and looked around me. I wasn't the center of attention. No one was watching me. I had a moment to take in my surroundings. The music pulsated in my ears as I watched well-built shirtless men dancing with each other like it was... well, normal. I had never seen anything like this before. It didn't bother me, and it didn't seem to bother Trina, but something changed for me. It was beginning to dawn upon me that there were men that felt just like I did. There were men who seemed to be happy being the very thing that society said was the worst thing to be. The key word being "happy." And on the bus ride home, my mind began to turn slowly. Were there other places like the Allegro? Were there guys who could like, perhaps even love, me the way that Trina did?

I pushed the thought out of my mind because to think about that would change my world completely. Trina couldn't be with me if I was going to find out if there were any other clubs like the one that we had been to. I didn't want to think about the repercussions of finding out what I secretly wanted to know but didn't have the balls to admit to myself. After all, if I could push Jason out of my head so easily, it would stand to reason that I could do the same with this new possibility.

The only problem was that I couldn't. I would lie awake in bed, wondering what it would be like to be among a group of men who would accept me for the very reason that society had rejected me. The idea of sex played a big part in this. As normal as I felt when I was with Trina, I still felt out of sorts. Even though I had forgotten about Jason, I hadn't forgotten how it felt to be touched by him. I never forgot how it felt to feel and kiss him. What resonated with me was the idea that I could have that close male friend and at the same time have the sexual companionship that I always longed to have. It was this thought that pushed me into what could only be described as "gay culture."

I make this sound so simple, like the idea of changing my life would be as easy as changing my socks or changing a record on a record player. In reality, it wasn't. It only sounds that way because it was the possibilities that compelled me to change my life. It took several trips to Center City alone and meeting a few people before I realized that maybe coming out would be the only option left for me.

I had met a young man downtown named Max. Our friendship had formed quickly and intensified in a way that I hadn't expected. I don't remember who introduced Max to me, but he stood out to me in two ways. Max was a hustler, someone that sold themselves for money. And yet I couldn't understand why he would do that because talking to him, I found him to be super intelligent. Max was biracial. From what I remember, he told me that he was black, Irish, and Puerto Rican. His eyes were dark, bright, inviting, and his outfits consisted of tight-fitting tank tops, shorts, and a baseball cap. I felt like I had always known Max... that he had been a part of me for years, but I couldn't figure out how. There wasn't a sexual interest in him at first. I really wanted to be friends with him despite the fact that he was excruciatingly handsome.

Every time Max saw me, he flashed a smile that could light up a city block, and when he looked at me, his dark eyes blessed with impossibly long lashes would make you feel as if you were the center of his universe. I felt his attraction to me instantly, but at the time, I really wanted to be just friends with him. Every time we saw each other, we would have conversations that would open our worlds to each other bit by bit. He knew about Trina but never asked me why I came down to Center City. I knew that he was a hustler and finally had to ask him why he did it.

"So tell me something," I asked him as we walked up Spruce Street.

It was warm that night. I remember that there was a light breeze in the air, and the street seemed to be alive with people going to the bars, nearby stores, and local restaurants. For all the activity going on around us, it felt like it was just Max and I. He walked with a steady, confident gait with a slight swivel of hips to suggest that he knew what to do when the time came. It was something that I noticed about him but put out of my mind because I couldn't allow myself to look at Max in any other way than just a friend.

"Sure." He glanced at me with a slight smile that played on his lips that only accentuated his mustache. At that moment, he looked like a teenage boy no older than me.

"Why do you do it?"

"Why do I do what?"

"Hustle."

"Dance?"

I shook my head with a smile. "No. The other kind."

He paused, looking at me with inquisitive eyes. We continued to walk up the block, passing by a woman who was out walking her dog.

"I don't know," he finally murmured more to himself than to me. "Nobody ever asked me that before. How come you want to know?"

"Because you're too smart for that."

Max went quiet. I could see the wheels in his mind turning. As we walked up Spruce Street, I realized that for everything that I had seen up to this point, Max didn't seem to fit. The streets seemed to hold a certain air of coldness that ran alongside the glitz and glamour of the disco strobe lights and dance music. Max seemed to be too nice. He didn't have the cold edge that seemed to be prevalent in the other hustlers that I had seen on Spruce Street.

"You think I'm smart?" he asked me, and for a minute, I was surprised. It was as if he had no idea how intelligent he was.

"Of course, I do."

"No one..." he began, and then he stopped abruptly. "No one ever said that I was smart before."

I was surprised. I couldn't believe that no one ever said this to him before. But then again, here he was, selling himself on the streets of Philadelphia for whatever dollars he could get. I never asked him what he charged for his services. I didn't want to know.

"Max, you are smart," I said softly. "I mean, I barely know you, but I know intelligence when I see it. I think you're smart … too smart for out here."

"Thank you."

I looked up at him and could see that his eyes were watering. I didn't know why.

"Are you gay?" he asked.

"Hmmmm?"

"Well, you're out here … talking to me now. I've met your girl-friend. Trina … right?"

"Yes."

"So are you gay?"

I thought for a moment. I had been accused of being gay in the past, and each time, it felt like nails going through my soul. I had fought most of my life to protect that secret. Now, here was a man asking me in all sincerity if I was gay or not. He was right about one thing though. I was with Trina, and I loved her. But if that were the case, how could I have found myself smack dab in the middle of a gay neighborhood talking to a man that I was … what? Attracted to? I wasn't sure. In fact, I wasn't sure about anything anymore. What was I doing? What was I looking for?

"Max, I don't know," I said after a moment's thought. "I don't know what I am."

I looked at him in the eye and saw that a tear had fallen, sliding slowly down his cheek. He stepped into me and kissed me, and for a moment, I felt myself responding to him. His lips were soft, his body chiseled and hard, pressing against me … and I was responding to him, my head a gale force of emotions and feelings. I pulled back from him quickly, seeing the look of bewilderment playing across his face.

"You can find out who you are … with me." He backhand-wiped the tears from his face. "We can find out what we are together."

"I don't think I can do that." I could feel my heart pounding in my chest.

"Why?"

"I just … can't." I turned away from him and started down the block. I had to get home to the safety of my neighborhood.

"Why?" he called after me.

"I just can't," I said without even giving him the courtesy of a backward glance.

As I rode home on the Broad Street subway, I kept thinking of Max and what he said. I thought of Trina, and I didn't know what to do. I had a decision to make, and I didn't know how I was going to make it. I didn't want to hurt Trina, but I couldn't see how this could be avoided. I wanted to find out more about this life I found, and I didn't have to be Max's boyfriend to do it. The one questioned remained, what was I going to do about my life now?

It entailed me coming out of the proverbial closet, first to myself, then to my girlfriend, and then to my family.

Telling Trina that we were over didn't go well and caused us both a tremendous amount of emotional pain. Our relationship ended in the middle of Rittenhouse Square in downtown Philadelphia. The day was warm, and the events that afternoon ring clear in my mind in some areas and fuzzy in others, dissipating and fragmenting the way that a dream does when you awaken. What I remember clearly about that day was the peach-colored blouse that Trina wore that day. Wide-framed sunglasses with a gradual tinting that went from dark at the top to clear at the bottom adorned her eyes. She had on a denim skirt and low heels. On this day, I had to tell her goodbye. On this day, I had to tell her that the reason that we couldn't be together was because I was gay, and that I had to find out more about who I was. By this time, I had discovered the gay community in all its decadent glory. I didn't know about the relationships that could be had, nor did I know about the normality of gay life. I knew the fun part … the clubs, the nightlife, and the possibility of being accepted by a group of people that were just like me. I didn't have to hide anymore, and I didn't have to pretend, not that I was ever pretending with Trina. I knew that it was time. I had to find out what this life had for me.

After telling her that I had to go my own way and that I couldn't take her with me, she didn't say a word. She was amazingly silent until two tears slid from beneath her glasses. What she said to me was heartbreaking.

"Now I won't have anybody to love."

I don't remember my response. I don't remember if we rode home together or not. I only remember that my heart ached heavily inside my chest. I had been with this girl who was now feeling the pain of a full-grown woman caused by me. She had loved me, and I had loved her, but now it was over. I wished that she would have screamed at me or maybe slapped my face. Her silence hurt me more than anything physical she could have ever thought of doing to me. Leading a double life with her never crossed my mind. It simply wasn't an option even though some of you may think that I did this very thing by being with Jason first and then being with her afterward. I disagree because I wasn't with both of them at the same time. My friendship with Jason, for as intense as it was, only lasted a few months or so. Trina lasted for a year, not including our initial friendship. Our relationship was more intense, perhaps because she was everything that I wanted in a woman if I were indeed a straight man.

And this brings me to another very important point in the coming-out process. If every man who identified himself as either gay or bisexual were allowed to be himself without fear of negative repercussions from their families, churches, and employers, there would be no need for any man to live a lie. A man would be either gay or straight. Bisexuality is another topic reserved for another book. I've always heard that bisexuality is just a rest stop to "gay town." That may be true for some men but not for all. I was raised to be a heterosexual man. I was raised to marry and have children regardless of whether it was in my DNA to do so or not. Most gay men were raised to be something that we either aren't ready to be or conform to, not because we want to, but because our society, families, and churches say so. It does not matter how we feel inside. It doesn't matter how many lives we may ruin while living a lie. And it certainly doesn't matter that we are desperately unhappy in marriages that are doomed from the start. To some heterosexuals, especially those from the old school of thought, being gay is the worst thing that you can be. To a man who loves and craves after women, how can the thought of being with another man intimately be appealing? The answer of course is that it can't. Heterosexuality is just as normal for a heterosexual man as is homosexuality for a homosexual man.

I don't want to get into the arguments of right and wrong, but I will say this. Regardless of what anyone says, you have to live your life in accordance with whom you see fit. If you desire a man, be with a man. If you desire a woman, be with a woman. What I think is wrong is trying to force someone to be who they aren't because in the long run, the damage done will be to that person. I've spent years trying to understand why I prefer men to women. I've questioned myself on more occasions than I care to count. What I've come to understand is that I have only one life to live, and I want to live it in peace. I am not supposed to be like everyone else. I am only supposed to be me...and in that, I have to be the best me that I can. I am not supposed to hurt someone or hide behind the facade of a loving family, knowing that I would be creating a place of discord, not only for me, but also for the woman that may fall in love with me and the children that she will bear. It's not only that it isn't right; it isn't fair. Meanwhile, heterosexuals are living their lives in the manner that they are supposed to...as they should. I will elaborate more on this in a later chapter.

Coming out of the closet wasn't easy. It had its high points and low points. It was both exciting and confusing, but I made it through discovering more about myself than I could have possibly thought of knowing. One of the most important things that I felt at the time was for me to find a partner, someone that I could share my hopes and dreams with. The next few years would prove to be uplifting and disastrous. Those years between twenty and thirty would be some of the most painful times for me. And yet I had to go through it to become the man that I am today. Throughout the entire period, my emotions ran high. They ran high for so long that I am personally surprised that they didn't burn out.

Little did I know that because of what I had gone through earlier in life, the stage had been set. My need for love and acceptance also meant that I would compromise my values to be with the man that I wanted to be with. It never occurred to me to wonder why any man that would claim to love you would demand that you change from the person that you were to the person that they wanted you to be. Hindsight being what it is, I found that as each relationship began and ended, I learned more about what I was willing to accept and deal with as much as I learned about what wasn't important at all. I learned about my must-haves and game changers, and like it or not, the eighties was going to be a tumultuous time. I would live the stereotypical gay life as well as allow my life to spiral into the depths of addiction. I would be tested over and over again until I began to pass the tests. But it took some time... and at the age of seventeen, time was all I had.

FAMILY

Being the oldest of four boys wasn't easy. As I've stated before, children don't come with manuals, and the oldest will always be the one that the parents will make mistakes with. My younger brothers and I maintain a certain closeness that I treasure. But it wasn't always like that. My two youngest brothers, Chris and Lynn, were more forgiving than the brother that was just six years my junior. He perhaps took my gayness the hardest and in certain ways made it more about him than me. To this day, I think that he was embarrassed of and for me. We had a volatile relationship up until the last ten years. Prior to that, I thought that I would never forgive him for some of the things he did and said to me.

Chris and Lynn buffered him and made it somewhat easier for me. But none of them knew of my history. They didn't know what happened to me earlier in life. How could they? I hadn't shared that with them. As a matter of fact, up until recently, I didn't share it with anyone.

My family is unique in the aspect that when I made it known that I was gay and didn't act ashamed of my sexuality, it made it easier for them to accept it. Not once did I ever get the impression that they had stopped loving me. There may have been periods where they were disappointed, but I know that I didn't experience the blatant rejection that some other gay men experience when they come out of the closet.

My brothers have met all the key players in my sexual development. They met Cherry, Jason, and Trina as well as my previous partners mentioned later on this book. They were not aware of the sexual relationships that I shared with these people until they came of age and understood the basics of human sexuality.

I mention my family because some of you may be wondering what it was like for me living first as a presumably straight man and then coming out of the closet. Coming out of the closet was liberating and life changing... literally. My world had expanded outside of the one that Trina and I had created. Some family members didn't understand how I could go from loving Trina in one moment to loving men the next. They didn't have the "filler" and didn't know the whole story, and I wasn't prepared to tell them.

One thing that I will say is that I was able to bring home each one of my partners because my family knew that if I did that, the person was obviously of some importance to me. What they said to my face was one thing. What they said when I wasn't in the room could have been something completely different.

Since I wasn't raised with my father's side of the family being in my life, I focused on my mother's side. My aunts, uncles, and cousins were particularly close, which in retrospect made it easier for me to be me.

I had cousins that were more like my brothers and sisters than siblings related to me because they were the children of my mother's sisters and brothers. I used to spend most of my weekends with Laverne, Aaron, and Simon. Aaron and Simon were close to me because they were in the same age as me. Laverne was a few years older. My memories of them were nights spent watching *the Late Show* followed by the *Late, Late Show*. We would have monopoly or pinochle tournaments until the wee hours of the morning and spent much of our time laughing like kids do.

This part of my childhood was what I considered to be normal, and none of them knew about the abuse that I had suffered. I never told them, which is odd because we shared so many secrets, you would think that what happened with Stan, Mr. Jackson, and Zeke would have been something that I would have told them.

Still, when someone is groomed to keep secrets, you do it. It never enters your mind to tell anyone. Even when Zeke kept me out all night long, I never told them what happened. My mother may have told their mother, but to my knowledge, none of my aunts ever shared that incident with them, and consequently, no one ever asked me what happened to me that fateful night. It was as if that night never happened.

Having a loving family can often be deemed as a two-edged sword. In one aspect, you have people that will love you unconditionally, at least until a condition comes up that they aren't equipped to cope with. My family knew Trina very well. She was firmly entrenched in my family as much as a girl could be entrenched in the lives of the boy that she loves. And I suppose it was in this particular circumstance that my family found it hard to fathom why Trina and I broke up.

I am sure that the person with the most questions was my mother. She had always considered Trina her daughter. I had to remind her on more than one occasion that Trina wasn't and would never be. She was probably the most disappointed and had even confided in me later in life that she often prayed that I would find myself a wife to finally settle down with. I believe that my mother was fearful of what would happen to me both now and as I got older. She was afraid of the ostracism that I would receive once I made it known that I was gay. She knew that her black son would have it rough in a world where being a black man was challenging enough. When you added being gay on top of it, she knew that I was in for a world of hurt and loneliness. It was a hurt that she couldn't protect me from, and I am sure that on many levels, that broke her heart. No mother worth her weight in gold would want to see her child suffer. I'm sure that she thought that life would be simpler for me if I married and had children the way that most straight men were supposed to. How could she know that doing that very thing would have complicated my life on so many different levels and devastated the lives of my wife, myself, and my children?

Being gay takes guts. It goes against everything that society says that we should be. At the time, I didn't realize how strong I was in taking the step to be the man that I had always been. Some gay men will never know this. They will continue to try to be the man that their families, churches, parents, and peers say that they should be, without ever embracing who they truly are because they've been taught that who they are is wrong. To live like that must be heart-wrenching because you believe that something is so inherently wrong with you that you have to change it at all costs, even if it means lying to yourself as well as to someone else. I can't imagine living like that, and yet millions of men do it every day. Despite all the advances in the rights of the LGBTQ community, there are men who would rather live in the shadows of themselves, pretending that they are everything except for who they really are. The idea of being "out of the closet" terrifies them, and for good reason. They stand to lose everything if they make that one confession. They could lose their homes, income, and families as well as their place in society.

For some, the idea of losing family is more than they can bear. It is easier to remain in the closet than it is to hope for something better. Some men couldn't begin to imagine bringing their preference to the light of day because it poses a direct conflict with what they've been taught since they were little boys.

I can't speak of that because that wasn't my reality. My mother didn't reject me when I came out of the closet, and neither did all my brothers. Admittedly, there was an "adjustment" period that needed to occur, but what I found was that the more that I acted as if I were ashamed of who I was, the greater the push I received against being and living my truth. Once I held my head up and acted as if I not only accepted my gay identity, but embraced it, it made it all the more difficult for my family to make me feel bad about me. It took me years to realize that this same concept extended beyond the family circle. Had I not want to belong to every social circle that I found myself in, my sexuality would not nor should it ever have made a difference... unless of course I was trying to make you my partner.

As the years went by and my brothers realized that I wasn't going to meet a young lady and "change teams," they began to understand that my relationships weren't any different than theirs. Each one of us had someone in our lives at one point in time that was not the right fit for us. My brothers have held window seats to all my relationships... the good, bad, and the ugly. They've seen me at my best, and they've seen me at my worst. At the end of the day, their love for me has never been diminished by my choices. Well, let me correct that... It would have been diminished had I remained in the bad state that I had been in and tried not to do anything about it. One of the things that I know for a fact to be true is that once you make the decision to come out of the closet, you open yourself up to a lifestyle that most heterosexuals either don't or refuse to understand. Straight men only know intimate relationships with women. They have no idea what it's like to be gay, nor do they desire to do so. As a result, it makes it easy for them to develop a sense of superiority no matter how distorted it may be.

Where a straight man may have to deal with fighting for their rightful place in society depending upon their race, men of color that are gay may have to fight twice as hard. Sometimes we win those fights; sometimes we don't. But most times, the fight begins within our own families. I fought to defend everything that I was as well as everything that I wasn't. I didn't want to lie, but sometimes, lying was just easier. Knowing what I know now, I realize that I was never ashamed of who I was as much as I just didn't want to exist on the outskirts of my social circles. My brothers made it easy and difficult for me to be me at different times in my life. The difficult times have been forgiven... but not forgotten. As time moved forward, the hurts inflicted, however deliberate or not, diminish, but they never fully go away. Sometimes, all it takes for the hurts to come back full force in the space of a second could be a harsh word. It has happened. And when it does, you have to fight to forgive and bury the hurt again. But sometimes it lurks just beneath the surface like the fast-moving current in a seemingly calm riverbed.

Today, I maintain good, solid, healthy relationships with my brothers. The youngest looks up to me despite the fact that he towers over me in height and outweighs me by thirty pounds. We maintain the closeness that a younger brother and older brother should have. He has been supportive in thought and deed. The middle brother, Chris, maintains a positive relationship with me that is enveloped in laughter. The brother following me has surprised me the most. As I recently stated, our relationship was volatile at one point in time, but he has become an outstanding husband and father. In so many ways, he has become everything that our biological father could not.

As for the rest of my family, they all know that I love them. All of them have, at various times in my life, made it easier for me to be me. And at the end of the day, that's all I could ask for.

FAILED RELATIONSHIPS—CHET

In order to love someone else, you have to love yourself. I didn't learn this until later in life. Someone that truly loves you would never ask you to compromise who you are because that is probably what drew them to you in the first place. What I've discovered is that men do it all the time, both gay and straight. I was primed to be whatever the man that I fell in love with wanted me to be because I wasn't strong enough to hold true to my own moral convictions. At this stage in my life, I wanted to please. I thought that if I gave him what he needed or became what he wanted me to become, he would give me what I needed. Sadly, in many relationships, it simply doesn't end up this way. As I've said before, and I will say it again, my emotional self had been altered with that first touch. I had been groomed by pedophiles at the age of thirteen. That was only six years prior. I was nineteen now. I had struck out on my own and felt at the time that I was old enough to make my own decisions. I knew what I wanted, or at least, I thought I did. I wanted to be loved by someone that could love me the way I needed to be loved. I wanted someone who would be in my corner, and together we could build our lives as we saw fit. It didn't matter the race of the man. It only mattered that he treated me well. By this time in my life, I wasn't aware of what roles men played in relationships with one another. I didn't know about the terminologies of "top" and "bottoms." But it didn't matter.

I met Chet at a dance given at the Center for Gays and Lesbians. I wasn't nervous when I went, and I don't remember how I found out about it. I just remember going, and during the course of that evening, a young thin white man with a thick mustache and hazel-brown eyes introduced himself to me. He had dark hair and was handsome in an offbeat kind of way. But he was nice enough that I wanted to spend time with him. Nothing happened between us that evening with the exception of the exchange of telephone numbers and a few nonalcoholic drinks.

But I was enamored with him. He seemed like a nice-enough guy. He was someone that I wanted to get to know. And so began my first gay relationship.

Less than six months into the relationship, Chet had suggested the idea of having a threesome. And when he did, it truly pissed me off. We argued about it heatedly whenever he brought it up—which was frequently. I couldn't understand how anyone who claimed to love me wanted to share me with someone else. But his ideology was that if we slept with other people together, we would never cheat on each other.

That wasn't necessarily true, but it worked for the moment. And in that, our relationship went from a twosome to a threesome. We began living the life of what some parts of society would consider to be the stereotypical gay. We lived in gay clubs, bookstores, cruised the streets looking for potential partners. It never occurred to me to think that my being younger than Chet would make me a "bait." It never occurred to me to think that because Chet was white and had an intense craving for black men, that I was the lure to bring these men into our lives and subsequently into our bedroom.

I would be lying if I said that I didn't enjoy the sex at first. I can't blame Chet completely. There couldn't have been a threesome if there weren't willing participants. But at one point, I had to ask myself if I would be sleeping with all these men if I were single. The answer of course was no. And if that was the case, why was I doing it now?

My early twenties was a blur of dance clubs, drinking, marijuana, and sex. We didn't think about the possible repercussions for the actions that we were taking. We smoked weed incessantly. We would walk down the streets puffing on a joint as if it were a regular cigarette and didn't care.

Chet had come up with the idea of selling marijuana so that we would have what we wanted to smoke for free. I followed behind him, not thinking that at this point, I had no plans for my future. I didn't think beyond the moment. I only thought about grasping to and living in the "happily ever after." I didn't realize that in the course of me reaching for happiness, I hadn't grasped it at all. My fingers didn't even graze the outer shell of true joy. I didn't realize that I was falling before I even took off into the sky of my life.

We had moments when we were truly a couple. There were times when I was sick, and he cared for me. We didn't always spend our time in the bedroom even though when I look back on it, it certainly seemed like we did. He wasn't always the man that couldn't get enough of sex. It's just that between his insecurities and my immaturity, I had to make some decisions about me, my life, and what I wanted in it.

I had compromised who I was to be with this man. He wasn't even the man I fantasized about. But along the way, we met one man that was. By this time, I was twenty-two or twenty-three, and Chet and I were still doing what we normally did. There wasn't that much happiness in our relationship as much as it was a weird type of codependence. Chet was terrified of being alone. He had more emotional issues than I was equipped to deal with, but I didn't realize it at the time. It began to dawn on me that maybe this wasn't the love of my life. Maybe he wasn't who I should be with because all our relationship amounted to was sex with people we didn't know. My going out without him terrified him to the point where he would be reduced to tears, and he would literally beg me not to leave. I don't know what he thought would happen. My guess would be that maybe I would meet someone that I would prefer to be with more than him. The irony in all that was in his willingness to share me with anyone who looked good; those very actions would ultimately lead to the very thing he feared would come to fruition if we continued down this path.

One of the last men that we had been with was a man that we had met out by Philadelphia's Art Museum. I noticed him right away. He was tall, extremely muscular, and by muscular, I mean bodybuilder muscular. His chest, arms, shoulders, back, and abs appeared to have been carved out of granite. He was walking along the park on a very warm summer day wearing blue jeans, biker boots, and a dark T-shirt that hung out of the waistline of his pants. When our eyes met, something ignited … and Chet saw it. To this day, I believe that in Chet's mind, this would be an ideal candidate for us to bring home since the physical attraction was so apparent. But when I looked at this man, I almost went deaf. He introduced himself to us with a very distinctive Irish accent. And even though Chet was there, for that moment, he almost ceased to exist. This man's name was John. That's all I remember, and that's all I cared about.

We rode back to our home in John's pickup truck, and once we arrived, we got out of our clothes, and I tuned Chet out. I liked everything about John … from the color of his honey-colored eyes to how gently he spoke my name. Sex was careful, gentle, and loving. There was more intimacy with John in that hour than there had been with Chet in all the years that we had been together. And it was in this that I realized that I wasn't in love with Chet anymore. I couldn't be if I could be with John so intimately. For the first time in a long time, I felt emotionally safe.

I am not by any means glorifying free sex. I'm merely stressing that this was the breaking point for me. Chet and I were over. We had been for quite some time; I just didn't realize it until that moment because in that moment, I wanted to know more about this man than time would allow. I wanted to know what was going on in his head. I wanted to know what drew me to him so intently as well as what drew him to me. Sometime during the exchange, I had given John my work telephone number, not thinking that he would ever call, but secretly hoping that he would. Chet knew that it was over between us, but I believe that he didn't know what to say or do about it. It took me a long time to open my eyes and truly understand that the relationship with him would take me down because truth be told, it already had.

I had sacrificed myself willingly for a man that didn't want love so much as he wanted a partner. He didn't want to live life alone. He wanted to have someone that would enjoy indiscriminate pleasure as much as he did. And with hindsight being twenty-twenty, what I realized later on in life was that we weren't so much a couple as much as we were co-conspirators. I wore that hat for a few years and accepted it. There were things that I did that I'm not proud of, but I realize now why I did them.

I wanted someone who had the strength to protect me. I also wanted someone who would allow me to protect them. There was never a battle as to who was stronger in the relationship. I ultimately knew that Chet was never going to be that person. It was with this knowledge that I packed my things and moved home to my mother's house to start all over again. But with the knowledge of John now nestled in my back pocket and the end of this relationship, what really sealed the fate of Chet and I was Omar.

OMAR

By now, the relationship with Chet had ended, but we were still friends. Even though we couldn't make it as a couple, we still hung out on occasion. I was twenty-three now, and I had a clearer idea of what I wanted in a man. I couldn't be with someone that could share the person that he loved as easily as he could drink a glass of water. That wasn't love to me.

Admittedly, I had become jaded toward white men in general and Chet in particular. I had sworn that I would never date another white man again, but what I was really saying was I never wanted to date anyone like Chet again. I had a certain amount of anger at him that wouldn't surface until later in life. But at this moment, he was my best friend by default. When I made him my partner, I focused all my energies into my relationship. I didn't allow room for basic friendships, and when the relationship with Chet fell apart, I didn't have anyone to hang out with, much less talk to about it. Some of you may be asking what my failed relationship with Chet has to do with being a sexual abuse survivor. Well, I was living with a need for acceptance thrown out of whack. Even when I had it with Trina, I was too young to understand what it truly meant to give of oneself completely and unselfishly. Most teenagers don't learn that until later in life.

Once I focused on an opportunity to be loved, needed, and wanted, it became somewhat of an obsession. Even though I knew that what Chet and I were doing was wrong on so many different levels, I still compromised myself to be with him. I bargained away my morals and standards (if I indeed ever had them at the age of nineteen.) Would this have happened if I had never been touched? After conducting some research and interviewing both male and female sexual abuse survivors, I am tempted to say that I probably wouldn't have settled for Chet. I would have had the emotional backbone to see that what he suggested, and eventually insisted upon, wasn't good for any relationship. With every man that we slept with, it pushed us farther and farther apart until we didn't have the basics for even a healthy friendship. At times, Chet made me angry, more times than I care to count. What I did was internalize all my anger and accepted Chet for who he was. This didn't stop him from making the occasional suggestion of sleeping with someone else even though we weren't in a relationship anymore.

Still, I wasn't a naive nineteen-year-old boy anymore. I was now a naive twenty-three-year old. And like it or not, I was getting ready to learn the hard way that compromising who I was wasn't necessary or needed.

We had stopped in a local bar for a drink, and in the midst of all the people present, a young man caught my eye ... and I caught his. In many ways, it was like meeting John all over again, only this time, the man was black. Every time I looked up at him, I found him looking at me, and I could feel the heat rise in my face. He was tall, dark, and intensely handsome. When he smiled at me, it was like he was shining a light deep inside my heart. Chet saw the eye connection and had made the suggestion that we go over to talk to him. I didn't say anything because I was tongue-tied. This wasn't about a threesome. This was about me meeting someone that I could be with, and it was starting off in the right way. Without realizing it, the man had made his way over to me and introduced himself.

Have you ever met someone whose presence could make you weak in the knees to the point where you had to fight to keep from saying the wrong thing? This is what it was like meeting Omar. He was charming, well-spoken, with skin the color of a Hershey's dark chocolate bar.

It was almost love at first sight ... almost. I didn't believe in that fallacy completely, but I was smitten. What was more important to me was that Omar seemed to be interested in me and only me. We exchanged numbers and went about our business. It took almost two weeks for him to call, and when he did, we talked for hours. He seemed perfect. But we all know that things aren't always as they seem.

People that are hapless romantics have a tendency to see and hear what they want to see and hear. They ignore the warning signs of a pending emotional disaster until it's too late. Gay men do it just as much as heterosexuals. If a straight man meets a gorgeous woman that he may consider out of his league, most times he will do anything he can to impress her and ignore the warning signs of what her true nature really is until he is in too deep. She may be selfish or insecure. He will overlook those things because there may be something about her that just draws him in. It's the same with a woman who meets a man who presents himself as being everything that she may have been looking for. He may paint himself as the perfect man until reality sets in ... and by then, she is emotionally invested, and it's too late.

Between my need for acceptance and my romantic side, I ignored the warning signs of what Omar's nature really was. I did it willingly because I wanted to believe the fantasy that was playing out before me. Sex wasn't going to happen with me or anyone else that I met the very first night, and any man that suggested it would be written off. It's not that I thought that what I had between my legs was outlined in platinum; I just felt that what I really wanted was someone that was opposite Chet. I wanted someone who could love me completely and allow me to love them back. But what came along with Omar was nothing that I could have prepared myself for.

Omar was sexy. He was six foot, the same height as me. We were very similar in build, and initially, I thought we had the same persona. One of our first dates was to the movies in the middle of the afternoon, and I remember him putting his arm around me as the movie played, which completely unnerved me. I got up very quickly and went to the bathroom because I wasn't ready for public displays of affection. I think that he thought it was funny, but I couldn't laugh about it. Not then.

For as much as I proclaimed to be proud of being gay, there was also the same amount of shame that came along with it. Meeting Omar was one of those whirlwind relationships that caught me completely by surprise, and before I knew it, I had fallen helplessly for him. But the storm clouds were gathering on the horizon, and it wouldn't be long before the typhoon touched down and would ravage my world.

Right before the relationship became serious, I received a call from John. I don't remember how much time had elapsed, but I was surprised to hear from him ... even more surprised that he remembered me. He said that he wanted to see me and asked me how I felt about going out on a date with him. I declined, telling him that I had started seeing someone new. The last thing that he said to me was, "Well, I tried." And I never heard from him again.

Still, for all intents and purposes, I was damaged goods. And just like I had done with Chet, I was now getting ready to make the same mistake with Omar. He had a way of gently demanding that you give him everything that you had to give while he reserved the right to withhold what he felt like withholding. Being faithful was never his strong suit, and I learned this very early on in our relationship. But he had done something that I didn't expect, much less saw coming. Without realizing it, I had allowed him to eliminate my support system. My brothers and what few friends I had were replaced with him. I didn't know it at the time, but the grooming process was happening all over again. Omar needed to know that he was the center of my world ... and for a time, I believe that I was the center of his. But that time was short-lived.

You see, Omar needed to be the center of attention. He needed to be regarded as the sexiest person in the room, especially when we went out together. The only problem was that the bars that we went to knew him well, but they didn't know me. This is where the contention started for him. Some of the guys would look at me wondering who the new boy was ... and it bothered him. On more than one occasion, our night out had been cut short because he became annoyed if someone looked at me too hard or for too long a period of time. It didn't matter that I was standing alongside him or that I didn't do anything to engage anyone at all. I think what bothered him was that someone was looking at me…period.

As I look back on this, I realize that there really wasn't any difference between me and a woman who fell in love with a man that would ultimately do her wrong. The arguments between Omar and me would become more and more frequent until it escalated into physical altercations. I realized that this was something that he was used to. Physical fights in his relationships were common. And yet it wasn't for me. I had become something that I never thought I would become. I had become an exact replica of him. He was a guy with thug-like tendencies, and I was becoming like him because I needed to survive. And yet this was something that I wasn't used to. I never understood how someone could think that physical violence within the realms of your relationship was okay. I never got that…until I met his family. Then, I understood that physical violence and infidelity were commonplace. The fights had escalated to knock-down, drag-out fights that often left us both battered and bruised. To this day, I wonder why all this had to happen. Why couldn't we talk out our differences instead of resorting to treating each other like a stranger on the street?

The weird thing about all this was that I loved Omar. I really did. And by the fourth year of our relationship, his cheating had escalated to blatant disrespect. I still loved this man despite everything that happened to this point. But Omar had become someone else. He wasn't the same person that I had fallen in love with. He had come up with more reasons not to see me and started keeping company with any and every one except me. The funny thing about all this was that a part of him had expected me to sit by complacently and wait for him while he did what he wanted to do with whomever he felt like doing it with.

On more than one occasion, we both suffered busted lips or bruises on our eyes because a simple argument had escalated to violence. He had a way of igniting passion and rage with equal intensity. I realized that I loved, hated, and feared him all at the same time. I feared losing him, hated his selfishness, and loved his passion. These were all new emotions within the realms of a relationship.

Once again, I had become something that I didn't recognize. Once again, I had sacrificed everything for love and acceptance. I had put to the side my need to excel in business. I knew that I had the gift to write but never pursued it because I was focusing all my energies on loving someone that was incapable of giving me what I needed. But this was only the beginning of my downward spiral. The worst was yet to come.

I was in my late twenties by now. I had been with Omar for almost five years, and yet I still couldn't see the forest through the trees. I was miserable, but somehow tried to convince myself that I was happy. Omar would come around, but it was more to check up on me to make sure that I wasn't seeing anyone else.

By this time, he had secured a job at a local college and had slipped on some water, which meant that he had to go out on short-term disability. Now he had all the free time in the world to see whomever he wanted to see, and if I heard from him on occasion, I was lucky.

Thinking back on all this, I wondered why I allowed my life to become so entangled with a man that clearly didn't love me. I thought of this repeatedly as I lay in a furnished room that I had rented for myself. Earlier, I said that I had made him the center of my world and assumed that he had made me the center of his. This was a partial truth. I allowed him to become the center of my world. I gave him that space willingly, and selfish people will take whatever you give them and demand more, making you feel as if you haven't given enough. I believe that people that fall head over heels with the wrong person experience this, and all truth being told, there is nothing that you can do to prepare yourself for it if you haven't gone through something like this before. You can tell yourself that if you ever meet someone so selfish, you would be able to recognize them at the drop of a hat and immediately cross them off your list and move on to something better. In theory, that sounds great. But for someone that has had their sense of self-worth damaged by molestation, what sounds good in theory doesn't work unless there is pain associated with it. My pain came from all sides. It came in the form of blatant loneliness. It came in the form of the one time that my brothers rejected me... not because of my gayness, but because in their eyes, my gayness led me to a man that took me so far out of character that they actually lost respect for me... at least at that point in time.

When I rented this furnished room, I met a young woman by the name of Sissy. She stayed in the room down the hall from me, and we became friends fast. I didn't realize it at the time, but Sissy was going to introduce me to crack cocaine. We had many conversations, and I enjoyed being with her. She was another voluptuous dark-skinned woman with long hair that for some reason or another, she never allowed anyone to see. She seemed to prefer wearing scarfs to letting her hair cascade over her shoulders. She had a bubbly personality with a quick laugh and a wit to match.

I had heard all horrible stories about crack. I had heard tales of instant addiction and brought these issues to light when Sissy had first suggested that we go for a run down to North Philly to pick up a "package." I can't pretend that I was this naive twenty-something-year-old that didn't know what he was getting into. I wish I could, but I can't. Being with Sissy in some ways filled the void that I had in my heart once Omar had left to be with whomever he was with at the time. The combination of being high and being with Sissy somehow eased the pain that I felt inside of me.

The scariest thing about all this part of my life was being around people that I ordinarily would not have kept company with. Mercifully, this lasted for a very short period. It only took a few nights of being up all night long with Sissy and then going to work the next day with no sleep for my world to come crashing down on me.

Omar was good at mind games. He was good at making you feel like you were the cause of all the problems in the relationship. And in my heightened state of anxiety, it was only a matter of time before something had to give... and it did. I lost my job, and since I had no income, I had to vacate the room that I had rented. I moved back home with my mother, feeling like a shell of the man that I used to be. Being away from Sissy, I didn't have access to the drugs that we had been using, which left me feeling even more alone.

If you could imagine your darkest day at any given point in your life, what was happening to me at this time was mine. There had been no closure with Omar and me. The love that I had in my heart for him was gone, which left me feeling empty. I may have been going through a form of withdrawal from the drugs. As I walked through the streets of Mt. Airy, I fought the urge to cry. I had never felt like this before or since and understood that I needed help if I was going to get myself on the right track. But I didn't know where to go or who to call.

As I headed toward my mother's house, I saw the front light on in front of St. Raymond's Rectory and headed right to it. I rang the bell twice, and I waited for someone to answer the door. A young priest opened the door, and I asked him if he could spare a little bit of time to talk to me.

Without hesitation, he let me in and guided me to one of the small offices inside. There was something about him that made me feel as if I was safe, and that it was okay for me to unburden myself. He looked at me with these intense blue eyes and asked me what was wrong … and I burst into tears.

"I want it to stop." That's all I could manage to say. "I just want it to stop."

He didn't say a word. Instead, he let me cry. I cried for fifteen minutes. It was like all the pain that I had experienced over the past five years came flooding out of me. I cried for the loss of my relationship. I cried for the loss of my confidence. I cried for the loss of my job and for the loss of the respect that my younger brothers once held for me. I cried because loneliness and I had become so intimate over this past year.

And without saying a word, this man stood up and came over to where I was. He put his arms around me, holding me close. There was nothing sexual about this gesture. He held my head to his chest and let me cry. He didn't say a word. I let myself fall apart at that moment. As the tears subsided, he raised my chin so that I could look at him in the face. I was surprised to see that there were tear streaks on his cheeks, and he asked me if I was ready to talk now.

I sat down on my chair and gradually told him about the last five years of my life. I told him about Omar. I told him about Chet. I told him about Sissy and the drugs. I told him how I had lost my job. And as my sadness subsided, a new emotion began to take hold of me. It was anger. It wasn't bright and hot like I thought anger should be. Instead, it was dull, like a piece of tinder that was stoked and ready to be doused with more kindling to bring the flame to a roaring brilliance that I couldn't have anticipated.

This was my turning point. This was where I would begin to start life anew. This is where I would begin my journey into finding out who I really was, and not what someone else needed or wanted me to be. My emotions were still out of whack. And it would be another twenty-three years before I would find out that everything that I felt wasn't something that should have been my normality.

DRU

If any heterosexual man has picked up this book and made it to this chapter, you may be asking yourself what my past failed relationships have to do with you. Well, it's simple; every relationship that you have experienced in the beginning of your life told you something about yourself as well as the other person involved with you. It doesn't matter if that person is male or female. Every time you ended a relationship, you came away with a clearer picture of what you wanted in a partner. If the woman was headstrong, and you are just as headstrong, maybe you wanted someone that is a little bit more docile or not as confrontational. If you are more laid-back, maybe you needed someone that would take charge and run your home and assume full responsibility for the children. The point is that every person that I had been with up until this chapter in my life helped to shape the image of what I wanted in a partner.

The thing that I didn't understand at the time was that I was, for all intents and purposes, damaged goods. My sense of self-worth was still out of whack as was my emotional state. I still had that overwhelming sense of wanting to be included, if not downright needed, but it would take me years before I could figure out why. At this point, I was still of the mind-set that the person I was at this time in my life was created by fate. There was nothing for me to link my need to please to. I thought that I was this overly needy man that didn't have the courage to stand up for himself. It didn't matter the image that I projected. On the outside, I appeared to be confident and in self-control. I thought that pursuing relationships was normal. What I didn't realize was that pursuing relationships became my reason for existence. It wasn't God or ascending the corporate ladder. I gave no more thought to how I was going to make my money than I did the clothes that I was going to wear the next day. For some of you, this may or may not have been your norm. You may see your reflection in some of my behaviors and thought processes. Some of you may be saying to yourself that you weren't that bad. Some of you may be saying that you didn't experience anything like what I experienced ... and that's okay. My point is that you may have similar experiences in emotional investments. Some of you may have escaped, not to relationships, but to casual sex; the more partners, the better. If you are heterosexual, the more women, the better. Some of you may have looked for something in the form of drugs or self-indulgence. Some of you may have pitched yourself into working hard, hoping that your efforts would be recognized by the "powers-that-be," and for some reason or another, it didn't work out the way you planned, so you continued to do the same thing over and over, hoping for a different result. I get it. I've been there. My personal story is simply to share with you what my life had been like. Up until this point, it hadn't been so good. But it would get better.

I met Dru at a bar called Key West. He was standing in a corner on the second floor about ten feet away from the dance floor. Was it love at first sight? No. But I was alone that night, and I felt like shaking off the day, so I decided to go out by myself. It wasn't my plan to meet anyone. It just happened. I don't remember who asked who to dance, but I remember dancing with him, and for the time being, I had forgotten about Omar and all the pain that he had caused me.

I was twenty-eight by now, and I was coming to grips with the fact that I was alone even though Omar called me maybe once a week or so. I am convinced that all he wanted to know was if I was home, and if so, if I was waiting on him. I was living with my mother and three younger brothers, and I felt okay. I wasn't great. But I wasn't the blubbering mess that had shown up on the rectory steps of Saint Raymond's church. Dru and I had shared a few drinks, a few laughs, and I was pleasantly surprised by how warm and cordial he was.

As the evening progressed, I realized that I had to get home so that I could go to work the next day. I had to take the Broad Street subway and then the Route 18 bus home, a ride that took roughly about an hour or so from Center City if I made the connections.

Dru walked me to the subway station where we talked some more and then exchanged numbers. I went home feeling light-hearted, not because I had met someone, but because for the first time in a long time, I didn't feel lonely. My brief stint with drugs was a memory, and I was ready for new friendships and new beginnings. If Omar called, I wouldn't take the call even though a part of me really wanted to talk to him. I still cared for him despite the fact that he let me down on so many different levels. Still, I couldn't bring myself to blame him for everything that went wrong with us. The truth is that a man can't do anything that you don't allow him to do. I couldn't be held responsible for Omar cheating, but I could be held accountable for staying. Love can screw your mind, and I suppose on so many different levels that I had let it screw mine.

I didn't realize just how damaged I was. I always thought that I was okay, and that loving someone else would come easily. What I didn't realize was that I didn't love myself enough to demand respect. I didn't love me enough to stand up for myself emotionally. Although I knew how to fight, the first time the physical abuse started with Omar, I couldn't bring myself to hit him back. In my mind, violence and love were two different things, that they should never intertwine. But as the violence continued to escalate, I realized that I would have to hit him back or get beaten … and getting physically beaten even by someone that I loved was not an option.

The first thing that I noticed about Dru was his intelligence. He was pecan brown, slim built, and he had the most beautiful almond-shaped eyes that I had ever seen.

Talking to him was easy. Being in his company was even easier. I was surprised how well we got along. We spent most of our time together laughing. And as days turned into weeks, which flowed into months, it wasn't long before our friendship began to shape itself into something more. I'm not sure who said "I love you" first, but I think that it was him. I say this not out of ego, but because Omar's shadow still hung over me like a black cloud. We had never said goodbye, which would have given me closure. Instead, we just drifted apart.

By now, I had moved out of my mother's house and into a friend's home in South Philly. We lived in a trinity townhome where he had the top floor, I had the second, and the downstairs was the common area. I believe that I lived there for a year before Dru asked me to move in with him. I was hesitant because even though I lived in this townhome for a little more than a year, I wasn't emotionally or physically involved with my roommate. The place was my safety net for the time being. If I moved in with Dru, I would be giving up my independence... or at least as much independence that I had at that point in time. But the more time that I spent with him, and the more he managed to push Omar into the back of my mind, I began to plan a future with him. I moved out to West Philadelphia and into a new life in a one-bedroom apartment to be with someone that I loved.

Dru became my best friend in every sense of the word. Our compatibility level was so high that it surprised even me. We began making plans to spend a life together. I had shown him my writings, which up until that point had been nothing but poetry, and he wowed me by reading every word. He encouraged me to continue to put my feelings into words as he was amazed by my raw talent. Up until this point, no one had ever encouraged me to write.

I don't remember meeting the editor of the *Philadelphia Gay News*, but I do remember meeting him for coffee. Lance was another person that was instrumental in starting my writing career. He had encouraged me to write an opinionated piece for the publication on my experience at a dance club located in Atlantic City. This particular establishment had questionable "carding" practices that didn't permit easy access to their club for African Americans. He thought that it would be good reading.

I wrote the piece, and it was published in the *PGN* within a week or so of writing it. I was bitten by the writer's bug then and have been writing pretty much ever since. It was also right around this time that I received a call from Omar. He wanted to spend some time with me, and I couldn't for the life of me figure out why. All I could do was ask him, not that his answer would have made a difference as I had been with Dru now for about half a year. But as I stated earlier, we had never experienced closure. He had heard that I was living in West Philadelphia, and he wanted to come and visit me. I politely declined, and when I did that, he wanted to know why. I didn't want to tell him that I was seeing someone new. I figured that if he had ever cared about me, then he would be hurt if he knew about Dru. Despite everything that he had done, I wasn't prepared to do that to him. But he pushed. He wanted to know why I couldn't see him. I think that he asked me this three times before I told him that my new "friend" wouldn't like it. He got upset and hung up the phone. I didn't understand why he felt the way he did at the time, but I do remember hearing a saying that may sum up how he felt. It goes something like this: "The most beautiful person in the world is your man/woman ... when they are in the arms of someone else."

I wish that I could tell you that it felt good to tell Omar that I was with someone else. I wish I could, but that would be a lie. Hurting someone has never been what motivates me. Revenge is not sweet, and it certainly isn't a dish best served cold.

Pain for pain isn't cool. It doesn't matter if the person deserves it or not. Revenge may feel good at the time, but it does nothing to enhance you. It doesn't make you better, and it certainly does nothing for the other person. In the end, if that person has hurt you, does getting back at them take away the hurt they initially gave you? If it does, then more power to you, but if it doesn't, why bother?

What I realized then is that I didn't hate Omar. I may have hated what he did, but I didn't hate him. I told Dru about Omar. I told him what he did and what had happened to me. Dru wasn't as forgiving as I was, and it wouldn't be for a few months before I found out the reason why.

Dru was as protective as he was possessive. I say possessive because he had a temperament that allowed little room for anyone else except me. He wasn't an insanely jealous type of individual at all. He was funny, quirky, intelligent, and handsome. And as I got to know Dru, I realized that there was a layer of pain that he had hidden from the rest of the world. He didn't have the best of childhoods, and as a result, he had to grow up quickly. He had told me the story of a time in his childhood where his class was going on a day trip, but he didn't have the money to go. He had come to school that morning and had to turn around and go home, and on his way, the school bus full of his classmates came to a stop at a light as he waited to cross the street. His classmates yelled out of the window for him to come with them, and he told them that he couldn't … and just like that, the bus rode off, leaving him to walk home alone.

Dru telling me that story triggered something in me. And I had made up my mind in that moment that I would give him back his childhood. In my mind, this was what he needed me to be. I know now that this is a by-product of what had happened to me when I was younger, but at that moment, I didn't know nor did I care. So the very first Christmas that we spent together, I went on a shopping spree for him. I purchased all the things that I thought that he would want and then some. I woke him up at the crack of dawn on Christmas morning and walked him out to the living room. He didn't expect anything like what I had done, and in that moment in time, I experienced the true joy of giving. I watched him as he looked at gift after gift, and then he looked back at me with a look on his face that I will never forget to this day. He asked me for whom all the gifts were. I said to him, "They are for you." He was overwhelmed. He didn't see that the best gift was a brand-new leather jacket that I had draped over most of the presents. This may have started the breakdown of any walls that he had built up over the years.

As time continued, we became even closer, and for once, loving someone didn't come with pain. And I found that it was easy to be this new person that Dru needed me to be. He encouraged me to write and clipped every article as it appeared in the *PGN*. It wasn't until years later that I found out that he had kept a scrapbook of all my work.

Dru had asked me to marry him within two years of our relationship. Even though the legalization of gay marriage wouldn't come for quite some time, it didn't stop us from formally tying the knot in the First Unitarian Church in Center City, Philadelphia. We got married in a small chapel wearing matching tuxedos complete with tails. The reception afterward was wonderful. One of our friends had given us a wedding present, which entailed going to Canada and staying at the Queen Elizabeth Hotel in downtown Montreal. And with all the positive things going on around us, I had no idea that our world was going to change drastically.

Years rolled by, and for the most part, Dru and I were happy. We learned how to cope with our finances, keep food on the table, a roof over our heads, clothes on our backs, and have a little left over to take in the occasional concert or play. As the years continued to flow like waters in a stream, the problems that most couples experience from time to time became more and more frequent. Sex was the main issue. If we didn't have it within a certain time, Dru would become angry and act out accordingly. The anger would sometimes lead to arguments, which would sometimes last for a few hours. But once we had sex, he would return to the loving person that I had fallen in love with. This created a bit of conflict inside of me. It was in the inconsistency of his behavior that I had to question whether he really needed me as much as I initially thought. Coupled with this was the realization that there were things that I needed to do that I hadn't done before. I had to go out and get my own apartment. Up until this point, I had never rented my own space. I had always lived with my partners, either moving in with them or getting a place with them.

My best friend and I were slowly watching our relationship unravel before our eyes. We started to pull away from one another. And yet despite everything that was happening, we never stopped loving one another. I think that at that point in time, we stopped *liking* one another. More and more, I began to wonder what it would be like to be with someone else. It seemed like the arguments were coming faster and more frequently than a pitcher trying to strike out the lead batter of the opposing team. We had forgotten what brought us together in the first place. All this led to me moving out of our two-bedroom apartment and back to my mother's house.

My time there would be short-lived as I had found a large studio apartment several blocks away from where Dru lived. This wasn't done intentionally. It just happened that way. I was comfortable in West Philadelphia. I had a part-time job out there, and even though I was struggling to make ends meet, I was happy at the idea that I had accomplished something that I should have done a long time ago. I should have gone and found my own place instead of worrying about finding someone who would love me.

I was living my own life, and it felt good. I furnished the studio apartment with great furniture, plants, and lamps that gave the place a distinct ambiance. It was something that I created, and I was proud of it. I missed Dru terribly, and I knew that he missed me. After I left our apartment and found my own place, we began to talk on a regular basis. My feelings about him were torn. I didn't want to go through the fussing and fighting about sex, but I was lonely, and I knew it. He stopped by from time to time to visit me, and we talked on the phone every day. One of the things that I remember most about my separation from him was the intense feeling of losing my best friend. Sex had poisoned something that initially started off as something so good. Back then, I couldn't understand why. But now I do. You see, in addition to my need to be accepted being thrown out of whack for me, sex in and of itself would never mean what it truly was meant to mean. As each relationship that I experienced ended, I believed that sex, whether it was in abundance, too little, or incorporated other people, always seemed to be at the root of their demise.

With Chet, it was bringing people into our bed; with Omar, it was his need for sex with other people; and with Dru, it was simply not enough sex between us. Sex slowly became something that I loved and hated simultaneously. Still, with all that, Dru was still my best friend up until this point. Losing him as a lover was painful. Losing him as a friend was unbearable. And as the phone calls continued with no animosity, I secretly hoped that we could make our relationship work. At one point, it actually seemed like we were on the road back to reconciliation, but one Sunday evening would change all that.

JOSHUA

Writing this book wasn't easy for me. I keep thinking that I should add this or that. I keep thinking that sex and drama sells, and if I have any aspirations of keeping my readers engaged, I should spice it up a bit. I also realize that to do so would be to take away from the message of the book instead of adding to it. I need to stay on point, and one of those points is to make sure that I keep the correlation between what happened to me earlier in life with what is going on in the present. Like I said before, many men don't believe that any damage was done to them by engaging in sex too soon—whether it is at will or not. I'm here to tell you that it makes a difference. It changes your psyche. You don't know the person that you would've become because your emotional trajectory has been altered. You may think that there was nothing done to you that you didn't want to happen. I'm here to tell you that you are wrong. A child cannot make a decision to have consensual sex. They are not emotionally equipped to do so.

I've hardened myself emotionally over the years because it became easier for me to survive. I've learned not to make the same mistakes twice, and each failed relationship taught me what I would and would not accept. I learned that bullshit came with both races. It wasn't the color of the man's skin that made him a good man versus being an asshole. It was the man himself who happened to belong to that particular race. Chet and Omar taught me that valuable lesson. Dru showed me that while we were the best of friends, there were things that I needed to do in life, and sex, if left to its own devices, can have devastating effects on a relationship if not kept in check.

I met Joshua in a bar on an unusually warm winter night. What made our meeting so unusual was that earlier that evening, Dru and I had gone to the same bar to have a drink and talk about us. We had agreed that it would be okay for us to start dating again since we hadn't made any progress on our reunion.

On this night, I sat at the bar talking to someone who was from Atlanta. The man was interested in me, but I knew that the most that could come of us would be a quick fling, and that wasn't what I wanted. I didn't realize it at the time, but I wanted something more. Joshua sat directly across from me. As a matter of fact, he was seated in the exact same spot that Dru and I occupied only hours before. The bartender initiated a conversation between Joshua and me, and before you knew it, the guy from Atlanta ceased to exist. Josh was sweet. That was the first thing that I noticed about him. The second was his eyes. His eyes were ocean blue, and his close-cut hair was the color of corn silk. I was struck by the way he talked. He came across as honest and sincere. In fact, if I had to summarize Joshua in a word, it would be "kind." He didn't come across as someone who was egotistical or self-absorbed. If anything, I was more self-absorbed than he was. I liked Josh from the moment that we began talking to one another. And it wouldn't be too long before we were seeing each other on a regular basis.

Our relationship started slowly at first, and in that, I found myself changing. Was it possible for me to be with someone sweet, kind, and decent and not have to worry about things that occurred in the past? After all, I had overcome a lustful past, an abusive relationship, and drug addiction. Was I ready for a monogamous relationship with Joshua? I would find out. We spent the earlier part of our relationship partying. I was in my early thirties by now, and Joshua was considerably younger than me. We didn't live in the bars as much as the bars were our primary means to socialize. One of the things that I did without Joshua was attend church. It wasn't that I didn't invite him. I told him that he was always welcome. I had joined a church a few years back located in Center City, Pennsylvania. It initially started with my lecturing (reading the selected verses from the Bible) during Sunday service. That evolved into joining the newly formed choir. And I loved this. This church had accepted me, and I quickly formed a bond with the Christian brothers that lived there. I had found a place where I fit in.

I remember hearing a homily given by one of the priests during one Sunday mass. This drove a particular point home for me. He said that "God loves us for who and what we are." That particular saying stayed with me. It was the first time that I heard these words connected with me. And I was grateful for that. It gave me a reason to sing. Even more importantly, it gave me a reason to believe.

Despite all my flaws and defects of character, I've come to understand that God truly did love me for everything that I was, as well as everything that I wasn't. I also realized that most of the problems that are inflicting our churches today have more to do with man than it does with God. I will delve deeper into that topic in a later chapter.

As my life with Joshua began to unfold, I realized that what drew me to him initially wouldn't be enough to keep me. His kindness was remarkable. Up until this point in my life, he was probably one of the kindest persons I had ever known. His kindness was only superseded by his generosity. What little he had, he had given to me and vice versa, and up to this juncture in my life, kindness in a man was definitely a plus given my previous experience with Omar and Chet. It was only natural for us to rent an apartment together, and after several months of dating, we did that very thing. We rented a one-bedroom apartment in Lindenwold, New Jersey…and for a while, all was right with the world. As the years rolled by, and we grew older together, I became restless. There was something missing in my life and in our relationship. I wasn't sure what it was initially, but I would find out eventually.

My relationship with Joshua was different in the aspect that I had no idea what to be when I was with him. I didn't know what he needed me to be, and conversely, since I was the very first relationship for him, he didn't know how to be with me.

I know that at various times in our relationship, he felt as if he had been shunned by his family. And it was in this shunning that he clung to me. Conversely, I was starting to find my own way. I started going to a gym on a regular basis, and that somehow led to my love affair with physical fitness.

But physical fitness and church were my own endeavors, and initially, Joshua took these activities as something that would take away from us as a couple instead of adding to me as a person. We argued about this, and many times, he lost. I think that he lost because I wanted to be something in addition to being his partner, and these activities allowed me the opportunity to do exactly that.

For once, I was allowed to be my own person, and admittedly, it felt good.

My relationship with Joshua lasted a total of eleven years, and its demise came for no other reason than my becoming emotionally unavailable to him. We had nothing to talk about. I was still drawn to his kindness, but I realized that kindness alone could not maintain a relationship. Consequently, he had to make the decision to move on with his life, and in retrospect, I couldn't blame him. He wanted something more than I was capable of giving him at the moment. But I realized one very important thing—I didn't need a man to complement or complete me. Don't get me wrong; relationships are nice, but at this stage in my life, it wasn't mandatory.

Now, you know how they say that when you aren't looking for love, that's when love finds you? Well, this is where I am currently.

MY CURRENT RELATIONSHIP

I wasn't sure if I would write about my current relationship, but in thinking about this, I am convinced that not including it would be an error on my part. You can't tell a story without some type of ending that makes sense. When you are speaking of failed relationships, there has to be something that shapes you into making better emotional choices. I wish that I could tell you that my current relationship is perfect, and that we don't experience our ups and downs. I could, but that would be a lie.

What I will tell you is this: over eight years ago, I met a man who was just as emotionally damaged as I was, although his reasons were not due to molestation. Our first year together was tumultuous, but not because of anything that he did or did not do directly. Our difficulties surrounded his circumstances, which I will not go into because it is not pertinent to where we are currently.

He has taught me many valuable things about myself, things that I would not have learned otherwise. I've learned that what draws me to a man isn't always the physical, but rather things learned in the course of a conversation as well as the experiences shared. Nice guys are not overrated. I found out that I love a man with empathy and compassion because this is something that the world needs more of. I also realized that although sex doesn't mean everything, it does mean something, and living a life with it greatly reduced in the way that you are used to doesn't always mean what you think it does.

I've found out that I have a very low tolerance for selfishness and self-absorption. I've also realized that it is just as important that a man allows you to treat him well and with respect in addition to him treating you good. I've learned this from my partner and friend.

I've also realized that communication really is one of the keys to the survival of most, if not all, relationships. So is the admission when you are wrong. There have been many times when I've been wrong and have had to "man up" and admit it to him. When I do it, I also tell him why my mind and heart went to a place that wasn't right to begin with. He understands. So do I because he does the same thing.

Are we perfect? No. Will we be together forever? I don't know because I don't believe in forever just like I don't believe in fairy tales. Would I like to grow old with this man? Yes, I would.

He has this way about him that is lovable. He is truly a loving person who needs me as much as I need him. He is as much a nurturer as much as he needs to be nurtured. He allows me to be who I am without compromise. He puts up with me as much as any man can, but there is something in his eyes that tells me that he loves me deeply. I say this because even though I know relationships are not perfect, and there have been many times when I questioned whether or not I wanted to remain in this one, I also know that what keeps me here is the fact that I am drawn to kindness, warmth, and tenderness. I love laughing, and we do quite a bit of that. We tell each other we love each other at least once a day. Is it a perfect love? No. But it's what has gotten me this far.

I've learned more about responsibility in the last few years than I have in my entire life. I have learned (and to a certain degree am still learning) that I have to be responsible in all my relationships whether they be personal or professional. He has been my rock when I thought that I didn't need one. In retrospect, I have been his. We have sought comfort in one another when no one else could provide understanding or empathy. We have had heated discussions under the most questionable of circumstances, but he makes it easy for me to come to him when I am calm and say the two most important words that a partner can say to another when they are wrong, and that is "I'm sorry."

It's not the fact that he is white that I love him. I love him despite of it. Actually, to be honest with all of you, I thought that my life mate would be either African American or Hispanic, if for no other reason than for the fact that they would understand my struggles as a person of color. After all, how could a white man who never experienced discrimination because of his race understand what it was like to be judged for nothing more than the color of your skin? And yet he does. It is in the many conversations that we have and will continue to have that endears me to him.

I wasn't ready for my partner who later became my husband. I wasn't ready for the kindness that he exuded because somewhere inside of me, I thought that I wasn't worthy of it. I thought that something was wrong because I didn't have to fight for my relationship the way I had to in the past.

Don't get me wrong; I had to fight for him. We had our issues, and there were times when I thought about walking away from him. But he didn't want to share me with anyone. He didn't want to be with anyone else but me. He thought that I was special, and he saw me for everything that I was as well as what I wasn't. And here's the catch and most important piece of this ... whatever I wasn't was okay. I was allowed to simply be me ... without compromise or explanation.

My family embraced him. He has become a welcomed staple with my mother, brothers, aunts, cousins, and uncles. They see why I fell as hard as I did for him. Would my mother wish that I would find a nice young lady to marry and love me like him? I'm sure she does. But will she accept my husband? I think she does because she sees certain characteristics in him that endears him to her just as much as it endears him to me. My mother knows that my husband loves his mother ... and right up to the day that wonderful woman passed to be with God in heaven, my mother knew. And that means something to her. My mother knew that when my husband's mother passed, that his heart had been broken, and a part of her wept for him. She had never been like this with any of my partners.

She knows that as long as I am with him, I will not grow old alone the way that she feared. You see, we've had conversations about this very subject. And while she will never truly understand being gay, she understands that her oldest son found someone that loves him and will look out for him.

I don't believe in forever. I only believe in for now. But I will hold on to this for as long as it is meant for me to have it and treasure it because life is just too short. I don't believe in shoulda woulda couldas.

CHRISTIANS

Everyone has to believe in something even if they choose to believe in nothing. I believe that nestled within every one of us is the need to experience an innate sense of superiority, whether founded or unfounded. In addition, I believe that we all have the need to believe in something greater than ourselves. Sometimes, those two factors embrace one another. At other times, they collide and in that create chaos where a sense of calm should reside.

At one point in time, I had subscribed to the postings of an African American news media outlet called The Root. In the past, they had brought up topics of interest for me in general as well as other African Americans, gay and heterosexual collectively. In one such post, the topic of what it must have been like to be gay in the south came up ... and of course, there were many responses, pros and cons alike. My comment was simple. I believed that God is the greatest form of love there is, and that if we were truly made in that image and were fortunate enough to receive love as well as give it, then we were mirroring him. My comment didn't so much have to do with the topic at hand as much as it was to offset the derogatory comments that were coming in. And right away, a woman commented on my remark. Her profile image was of her in her wedding dress accompanied by what I assumed to be her husband, and right away, she embarked on what I took to be an attack on my comment as well as my character. She wrote several lengthy paragraphs about my selfish pleasures, talked about how wrong I was to be what I was, and began to lecture me while spouting verses of the Bible to back up her message. She then ended her last paragraph with "Don't get me to teaching up in here."

I was so taken aback by her response that I wrote back to her stating that maybe she should teach as there may be people that could glean some wisdom from what she may have to say. I also pointed out that she may want to leave her judgment up to God since it clearly states in the Bible that it isn't her place to judge others at all. She responded back with a longer tirade, pretty much stating that it was her place to judge, just like it was the place of Christians like her to follow suit. I realized that there was nothing that I could say to her to change her thought process nor could I open up her mind. Whoever was teaching her in the realms of her church had taught her incorrectly because even I, without reading the Bible, am aware that you can't sit in judgment of someone else. In essence, you can't play the your-sin-is-greater-than-my-sin game and expect people to receive what it is you are trying to say. I ended my conversation with her by bidding her a nice day, and I stated that I didn't want to engage her any further. I wanted to enjoy the rest of the afternoon with my friends and significant other. I didn't need her to agree with me, and I certainly didn't need to agree with her. But if all we were going to do was go back and forth with our viewpoints and not be enlightened, then what was the point?

There are literally millions of Christians like this woman. There are millions of people who claim to know and love the Lord and will treat others with such hateful disdain that you would never know that they sit each Sunday in church and allow tears to flow from their eyes because they profess to love Jesus so much. I've read the Bible from cover to cover and continue to do so because each time I do, I glean a little bit more wisdom from its pages. I've come to realize that although I am fully aware of what it says about homosexuality in the book of Leviticus, I also realize that the source of this book is God...a loving God, a forgiving and trustful God, a God that I love, and I am convinced loves me for everything that I am as well as everything that I am not. This God's beautiful son died so that I might live. Nowhere in the Bible does it say anything counter that. It does not say that I will spend the rest of eternity in hell because I love another man. All it says is, "Thou shalt lie with mankind as with womankind; it is abomination." Now while I understand exactly what this passage says, I cannot change who and what I am. I will not hurt any more women than I already have because I wouldn't be honest with myself. I trust God in more ways than I can imagine, so I know that beyond a shadow of a doubt, no matter who I am, my God loves me. I cannot say the same for some people that follow God.

Many Christians who claim to know and love God will use this verse in the Bible to support and sustain their hatred of the LGBTQ community. Many pastors have preached on this very topic repeatedly. I have had many Christians who claimed to know God love me when they thought I was heterosexual, only to hate me when they found out that I wasn't. And what I personally believe is that many heterosexual Christians will use Leviticus 16:22 to support whatever intolerance they have in their heart. It almost appears as if I am supposed to love and marry a woman and live my life miserably, denying who I am in the guise of living righteously as opposed to being who I am and living my life the way that I see fit. Either way, God loves me no less. And if this is indeed the case, why would I elect to live my life unhappy? That makes no sense.

I've often said that many a Christian who hates the people of the LGBTQ community had a hatred for the people of that community long before they read that particular verse in the Bible. When it comes down to that verse, some of them conveniently dismiss the fact that you are supposed to love the sinner and hate the sin, and since we are all sinners, what appears to be going on is that some Christians will pick and choose which sins they can tolerate and which sins they can't. The sins that they cannot tolerate, they will use the Bible as a means to justify how they feel instead of loving that person no matter what. I've stopped going to church because of this in part. I stopped because I needed to discover God in a way that I couldn't do within the realms of organized religion.

What I have to say to Christians is this: learn to love as Jesus has loved you. Before you go around telling everyone how much you love the Lord, learn to love the way the Lord you serve loves you. Do not be unkind. Do not be judgmental. Let God handle us because God already has. Look deep within yourself at whatever sinfulness you have and work on that. Don't stand in judgment of me and mine because there will always be someone that will stand in judgment of you and yours.

It takes a lifetime to love as Jesus has, so work on that because we all know that life is just way too short. I've often heard that sin is sin, and this is true. There are no degrees of sin. Therefore, if you are human, then you have sinned and will probably continue to do so. It is only by the grace of God that you are going to wind up in heaven. Instead of condemning others that are different from you, the harder thing to do would be to love them. It is far easier to be unkind in the name of God than to display God's love. It is easier to pick and choose what you will tolerate simply because you may or may not understand it.

There are many things that I don't understand, but simply because I don't understand doesn't make it right or wrong. I don't have the right to condemn anyone, especially with the mistakes that I have made in my lifetime. I believe that somewhere in the Bible, it says, "Lean not on your understanding." I find this to be true. I choose to work on me because dealing with my own issues is a job in and of itself. It lends little time to correct anyone else's behaviors. If you ask me what I've learned in life, I will tell you. If our conversations happen to stray into the realms of where I was as well as where I want to be, I will gladly share them with you. If you ask me about God, I will share that with you as well. But I will not stand in judgment of you because it isn't my place. The only entity who has the right to judge me at the end of the day is God.

Certain Christians baffle me. They claim to love God and abide in his/her word and walk in truth. And yet in their belief system, they denounce others who are different than them, perhaps even going to the length of making them pariahs within their own community...all in the name of Christ. But this isn't what Christ was, and this isn't what he believed; at least this is what I believe based in the scriptures that I have read.

Issues need to be addressed from the pulpit in addition to the word of God, issues that would complement his/her word. How many men would listen if a pastor preached how he is supposed to love, protect, and adore his wife as opposed to her being submissive to him? Can we address issues that are pertinent to the times that we are living in? Can we address issues like domestic violence and child abuse in the home and how we can overcome this in God's name? And can we leave judgment to God and God alone and stop trying to force people to be a mirror of who they are or would like to be, especially when that mirror image isn't so shiny behind closed doors? Can we bring unity to our churches and communities by making the doors open to everyone since not one person that walks through those doors is without sin?

When the Supreme Court ruled that it was perfectly legal for gay men and women to marry, many Christians lost their mind and espoused words that were both hurtful and hateful. In short, they were anything but godlike. But as I sit behind this computer writing this, I wonder how many of those pastors and members of the congregation know how many people that belong to the LGBTQ community attend services under the same roof as them? I wonder if they know or care if the tithes that they collect come from devout Christians that are of the same community as me, and if so, does it matter that that they preach hatred and intolerance from the pulpit in the name of God?

I hold on dearly to what I believe God to be. God is love, and I believe that he/she will not judge me with the same severity as man. God is God… period. God doesn't have a need to be better than the man that he/she created because the Creator is always better. It is man that needs to feel superior to his fellow man, and therein lay the hatred and bitterness that resides in his heart. Many of us fight to rid ourselves of this hatred, and some of us embrace it. How you deal with it lies in direct correlation to who you are.

Preach God's word. Preach from the hilltops. Just understand that God welcomes all his children… both the young and the old, black and white, gay and straight. When you condemn or exclude in his/her name, you are doing the total opposite of what God commands you to do.

In this world, we fight to belong. We fight to be exclusive. Sometimes, we fight just to exist. I cannot tell you how to believe, but if you are going to extol how much you love God, you have to be willing to be like Jesus and embrace everyone ... even those whom you do not understand.

I've since joined a church where how you walk is just as important as the fact that you walk. My belonging is voluntary and my presence welcomed. I have found out more about myself in the short amount of time that I have been a part of this church than I have in my entire walk within organized religion.

I still struggle with my humanity, but it is in that humanity that makes me who I am, with all its idiosyncrasies and imperfections. It is through my faith that I walk, take this path in life, and know that I am going to be okay.

Indeed, the hardest thing for a man to do is to forgive himself for the wrong that he may have done throughout his life. But I work on it day by day.

NOTE TO FATHERS

I believe that when you are born, the relationship that you share with your parents will fall into one of three categories. Assuming that you are a son, you will either be a mama's boy, a daddy's boy, or you will fall somewhere in between. Up until recently, I always thought that I was a daddy's boy. Despite all the wrong choices that my father made throughout his lifetime, I still idolized him in one way or another. I always wondered what it would have been like to experience being his son, and what I realize now is that what I idolized is and always will be pure fiction. I had to accept that he will never be the man that I thought he would be. He will never give me the answers that I need, answers that only he could provide.

Men like my father will minimize the damage of the choices they made as well as the effect that it had on the people around them. They have a tendency to rationalize that what they've done as being not so bad, or that perhaps their children were too young to really remember what was happening. My father is no exception. Although I love him, I know that had my parents stayed together, I would not have turned out to be the man that I am today.

My father would not have handled my homosexuality or my sensitivity well. Maybe I would have been beaten, or maybe I would have been thrown out of the house at a very young age. I will never know this, but when I look back on the track record of the relationships that my father's side of the family experienced with their own children, I have to believe that ours would have been no different. I've heard tales of one of my aunts throwing her daughter out to the street in the pouring rain, knowing that she had no place to go. I don't know the reasons why, but I still shake my head sadly as I believe that there must have been an easier way to resolve conflict with your daughter than to make her leave your home abruptly and without a safe place to call her own. I've personally heard the yelling and screaming that was indicative of my father's side of the family ... not saying that this is all they knew at the time or know presently. I do know that there is a deep sense of pain that resonates within most of those family members. And I know that true healing cannot begin until that pain is addressed and ownership is taken.

I wrote an article a while ago entitled "Whatever Happened to the Parents of the Baby Boomers?" In that article, I surmised that older men, men that would be in their early to midseventies by now, are experiencing a backlash of the lack of love and affection that they withheld from their children. They were taught to be the breadwinners as well as to lead and provide for their families. They were also taught to assume the role of head of the household, whether deserving or not. The role of nurturer was left to the mothers. Some fathers from that generation could not have been bothered with what they considered to be coddling or displays of affection. Even the very words "I love you" fail to fall from their lips and land on the ears of those that need to hear it the most. Many men from that era thought that their role as a parent was to punish and discipline their children whenever they thought they got out of line.

As these men grew older, they have become somewhat bitter. Father's Day and birthdays pass by with little or no observance in some instances while Mother's Day and a mother's subsequent birthday are celebrated. Had my father been my protector and behaved like a man who truly loved his son, it is possible that some of my molestations may not have taken place. You see, I was looking for my father in Stan. I wanted an older man to take interest in me. I wanted to do the things that fathers and sons did together. I wanted the Norman Rockwell picture-perfect version of a father. I would gladly have embraced the James Evans from the hit show *Good Times* version of a father because at least that man, with all his idiosyncrasies, loved his wife and his children.

While it would be easy to assume why my father wasn't there in my life when I needed him the most, the fact that remains glaringly obvious is that he simply wasn't. He wasn't there to guide me into my teenage years and later into adulthood. There wouldn't have been a need for a Stan or any other man to step into the role of parent if the role had already been taken by the person that it should have been occupied with from the beginning. I believe that my father didn't try to work at his relationships, not because he didn't want to, but because he simply didn't know how. Women and children had their roles clearly defined in his mind. Women were subservient, and children were to honor him. It was that simple... black and white with no shades of gray. He didn't have to try to be anything more than who he was. He didn't have to explain himself to anyone, not to his wife or his children, even if he were hurting them. That is who he is, and no amount of coercing will change that. He knew how to be a painful disciplinarian, even when he could have made his point with love instead of the belt. But the belt is what he knew.

It may sound like I am bashing him. I assure you that I am not. I have no idea who he is except for what he has shown me. And it became painfully clear that I would never get the answers that I needed in order to have a healthy relationship with him. He will never tell me if he thought about me or my younger brothers while he was only a state away living with a woman and her three daughters. He will never tell me why he didn't want his own family, even if it was his family that left him. Changing his behaviors, I'm sure, never entered his head... and if it did, he didn't entertain the notion for very long.

My father had the chance to make this right... many, many chances. He could have earned his place as the head of the household and been revered by his sons and wife, if only he had learned to put others ahead of himself. It seems to me that this may have been his problem all along. He always put himself first. He came before his wife, family, and children. It was his happiness that came first before anyone else. It was his comfort that took precedence in his life. I see that he was selfish then, and because of that selfishness, he has lost so much. You would think that I would feel sorry for him, but I don't.

I don't because I know that he refuses to change. The expectation is that everyone around him would or should change with the exception of himself.

What I have to say to fathers is this: when you have a child, you give up who you are at that point. You surrender your dreams temporarily because your responsibility has changed. You are no longer responsible for yourself. You now have a son or a daughter who needs you. This responsibility is to be shared between two parents, and it is not the mother's job to play both roles. Saying that things aren't right between the mother and you will never be an acceptable excuse. The role of a nurturer is not left up to the mother no matter what you have been taught or, in some cases, haven't been taught.

Your role as a father is to not only lead, provide, and protect; it is also to encourage and nurture with love, patience, gentleness, and kindness. It is also your responsibility to discipline when needed, but it is not your only role. You set the example because at the end of the day, your children will look up to you. Your children will honor you, but honor only comes to those that are honorable. If you want to be looked up to, then you have to behave accordingly. Any man can be a daddy, but only true men can be a father.

You have to listen to your children and let them know that they matter to you, even if the woman that helped you to create them does not. Children don't ask to be born into their circumstances. You help create those circumstances. Don't assume that the battering a child hears will go away as they get older. It doesn't. Children don't forget.

I still bear the emotional scars over choices that my father has made. With every action that he did, he indirectly told me how much he either did or did not love me. Simply because you have a son, and he is supposed to be tough, does not make him invincible. He will learn how to interact with people, women, men, socially and economically from you first. He will learn how to trust others from you. He will learn his first words and thought processes from you as well.

I say this because this has been my experience as well as the experience from other men like me. We have learned to hide our hurts and disappointments. We are skillful at blaming others for our shortcomings and mistakes. When I say this to you, please do not think that I am blaming you for every shortcoming that your children have or will experience. Just know that it starts with you. This is something that you need to own and accept.

Men do not ask to be gay. We don't think that this is going to be an awesome life for us when we are younger. We are already going through enough with the physical changes happening to our bodies as we become young men. We don't know what's out there in the real world until we are forced to deal with it. Our gayness isn't about you; it's about us. You may beat us, punish us, throw us out of the house, or turn your back on us, but it will not make us any less your son, nor will it make us any less gay. You cannot break a bond that has been made simply because we did not turn out to be the man that you wanted us to be. We can only turn out to be the men that God intended us to be. Either way, you still have to lead us and tell us that you love us regardless.

In turn, we will try our best to love and give you the honor and respect that you have earned. I say earn because that truly is what it is. You are not going to get respect simply because you lie down with my mother. You earn respect by being who your children need you to be.

There are things that you will not understand. You will not understand how your son can be gay when you've done all the right things and made the right choices. I don't have an answer for you because once again, your child's orientation has nothing to do with you. This is who they are. You can either make it easy for them, or you can make it difficult. Some fathers will choose the latter because they don't understand that their child's orientation has nothing to do with them being or not being a strong man. They will buy into the stereotype that their son is less than a man simply because he loves someone of the same sex. They will take their orientation and believe that their son will somehow be all the things that are wrong with society, not realizing that your son can be heterosexual and still be all the things that are wrong with society. Some fathers will make the mistake of making their child's orientation about them, and that somehow who their sons turned out to be translates to shame for them.

My father once told me that he was upset with me because I had told his live-in girlfriend what I was "into." In retrospect, I believe that they had a fight, and she threw my homosexuality in his face, and there was nothing that he could do or say. The one thing that I clearly understood was that their relationship had less to do with me and more about their dynamic, and at that point, they were looking for ways to hurt one another. In that instance, my gayness was a pawn.

On Thursday, September 3, 2015, I called my father after not speaking to him for over a year. I don't know what prompted me to call him because he hadn't been on my mind at all that day. I had never deleted his phone number out of my cell … and in retrospect, I'm glad that I didn't. He picked up on the second ring and sounded as if he was groggy, so I asked if he had been asleep. He told me that he was. I told him that I would call him back the next day because I wanted him to be wide awake when he heard what I had to say. He said that he wanted to talk, and so we did.

For about ten minutes, I told him everything that I had been meaning to tell him for the last forty years. I began by telling him that I love him and always would, but that I had missed him over the years. I told him how I felt about the choices that he had made, how he had, in effect, chosen to shelter and protect another woman and her daughters who were not biologically his, while his sons grew up in Philadelphia without him. I told him that I had no memories of love from him. The only memories that I had were that of his belt, extension cord, or strap. I told him that inside of me still sat an eight-year-old boy waiting for his father to come for him, and he never came. I told him that he had missed out on so many firsts … proms, first dates, getting a driver's license, and graduations all because he wanted a life that didn't include us. I also said that his sons grew up to be four talented, strong black men. There was more that was said because by now the words were pouring out of me like a river flowing over a waterfall. There wasn't any anger in my words … just simple statements of fact. I needed him to hear what I was saying and not hear my anger. What he said afterward surprised me. He said that his health had begun to fail him and that he wasn't doing very well. He said that prior to my call, he had been reflecting over his life and had deep regrets over the choices that he made. And then he apologized to me. He said that he was sorry for all the pain that he had caused this family. He told me some things that I already knew, like how he was never taught how to love. He only knew beatings, and that was what he grew up with.

I had to hang up the phone at that moment and go to my bedroom and cry. I cried for the time lost. I cried for his health because I knew that age and loneliness have a way of creeping up on you when you least expect it. It forces you to look at things that you might perhaps never see. I don't know where my father and I will go from here, but I no longer feel the need to cut him out of my life. You see, I finally got my answers. I knew that he didn't think about his sons in Philadelphia while we were growing up. I knew that he was blinded by what was in front of him at that time in his life. He needed all the superficial things that he thought would make him happy, but not the lasting, enduring things like a loving wife and the adoration of his children.

I wanted you to know this because there are many men like my father. There are men that will use the excuse that things didn't work out with the mother, so therefore they forget the children too.

But the good thing about life is that it is full of choices. You can choose to make the wrong choices in life, or you can make the right ones for once. You cannot reclaim the past, but you can begin anew. You don't know what the future holds, but you have today. That is why it is called "the present." It's a gift. It's up to you as to what you do with it.

All the struggles that I have endured over the years have ultimately made me stronger, not in every way, but in the ways that matter the most. I have learned how to love and not dominate. I have learned that even at this juncture, I still have a long way to go.

I hope and pray that I never wind up alone and, consequently, lonely. I don't know what is ahead of me, but I do know what is behind me. My beginnings... as humble as they were, it could have been so much worse.

But the one thing that haunts me periodically is, what kind of man would I have been had my father been there? Would he have been the man that he is now, or would the love of a good woman and the adoration of his sons softened him? Or would he have been tyrannical... perhaps demanding respect where respect should not be given?

We will never know this.

I do know that at least one of my brothers has had this conversation in his own mind and now wants to have the conversation with my father. He has turned out to be a wonderful man, excellent husband (at least as far as I can see), and a loving parent. I don't know how my two other brothers feel, but I imagine that they may have simply written our father off. I'm not sure of this, but I can only speculate.

The one thing that I can say with extreme clarity is that a father's role should never be underestimated... least of all by the father himself. Your children will need you. It is up to you if you choose to fill that need.

NOTE TO MOTHERS

The role of a mother has changed over the years. In many homes across the country, homes are headed up by the mother. To many of you, I take my hat off. Many of you are doing everything you can to make a better life for yourselves and your children. Some of you are not only raising your children alone, you are also going to school, going to work, and running your homes. For many of you, there simply aren't enough hours in the day to tend to every single one of your children's needs. You are lucky if you meet three-quarters of them.

While you are out there being supermom, one thing that can't be neglected is your children's emotional well-being. To find out the truth means setting aside time with your child to have those conversations that may exhaust you before you even open your mouth. Just understand that your child won't tell you everything...at first.

A groomed child has been taught to keep secrets, even at their own expense. Part of your job as a mother is to uncover these secrets and hopefully stop the abuse. I say hopefully because at times, it may be easier to dismiss the idea of anything happening when evidence may state otherwise. It is easy to blame your child's mood swings or changes in behavior on becoming an adolescent. That may indeed be part of the problem. But there may be more to the story.

I may not have been ready to tell my own mother about the abuse that happened with my uncle or Stan, but I was ready to tell her about the abuse with Mr. Jackson. She thought that maybe he looked at me as a son. I didn't know how to tell her how wrong she was or what this man was really doing to me, so I let it go. I let it go because I knew that if the abuse were perpetrated by a man that I thought was attractive, I wouldn't have said a word. But then again, this is what goes on in the mind of a groomed abuse victim.

Could my mother have done something to prevent this? Probably not. My first encounter with a man was at the age of six. The second was when I was about thirteen. By then, her hands were full trying to raise four boys alone while dealing with her own private issues. When she realized that something was wrong, she did her best to intervene by taking me to see a psychiatrist. I know that she did the best she could. I don't hold her at fault for anything.

Still, there are things that you can do as a mother that may help the situation rather than exacerbate it. When Zeke kept me out all night long, I tried to tell my mother that I had tried to call her. I tried to tell her without naming Zeke initially that he had called a cab for me. None of this worked. She was probably flooded with relief that I wasn't out in the street lying dead in an alley or abandoned house. And still, she was also flooded with the second emotion, and that was pure anger that I had deliberately disobeyed her. There was nothing that I could have said to convince her otherwise. There was no excuse for the disobedience, and the only response to disobedience was punishment.

As a mother, you will be faced with actions that your child has done. Some responses will be quick and easy; others will require thought. Just understand that sometimes, a child does something, and your natural reaction may not be the appropriate reaction. At age six, when my mother caught me with Tim, she was right to tell the boy to leave. But the next step should have been to ask me where I learned to do what I was doing.

I don't know what I would have told her. Maybe I would have told her that I learned it from my uncle had I not seen the rage in her eyes. Rage causes children to retreat into themselves, or it may cause them to lash out. Rage makes them feel as if they are at fault. Either way, you won't get the information that you are looking for if your reaction to their behavior is in the extreme. Admittedly, it may be hard for you to contain your initial reaction, but in order to find out the truth, as painful as it may be, you have to put aside your natural reaction and focus on your child. They have to know that in no uncertain terms that it is safe to tell you whatever it is that they have to tell you, and whatever they say, you cannot or will not blame them.

My mother asked me about my relationship with Stan. I denied it vehemently because I was protecting my relationship with him. A groomed child will do this. A groomed child will lie for their perpetrator, and the reason why they will do this is because the pedophile has gained your child's trust. Once that trust has been obtained, it will be equivalent to moving Mt. Everest to convince that child that something wrong is taking place, and that the person that they have placed their trust in is indeed hurting them. You may want to scream, shout, and shake your child into reality, but it will not do any good.

The world can be a scary place. It is a place where children grow up healthy and whole, but it is also a place where things happen ... scary things. You as a mother have to know where to draw the line between being protective and overly protective. It's a fine line to walk, I know. It's challenging. You don't know when to let a child go and just be a kid with all their curiosities and wonderment.

Listen to your child, and then trust your instinct. My mother's instinct about Stan was spot on. But it was blind when it came to Mr. Jackson, and she knew absolutely nothing about Zeke who was the most dangerous pedophile of them all. Keep the dialogue between you and your child open. Being a mother means being your child's friend of course ... but it also means being a parent first.

WOMEN

I've had experiences with girls and a few women. In terms of honestly loving a woman, I think that I loved two in my lifetime. Cherry was my first love because she was the first girl that I actually interacted with even if I didn't know how to interact with girls properly. The second was Trina. By the time we met, I realized that in order to fall in love with a girl, I had to like her. Trina and I became friends. Despite the fact that I held my feelings about guys at bay and away from her, loving her was deliberate; my hurting her was not. Some of you may disagree... especially women. What I will say is that you are looking at my relationship through your own lens as opposed to the lens of the person that I was at the time. Your lens and mine are completely different. I didn't know about being on the "down-low" any more than I knew that there existed a community of men and women who were exactly like me.

You may think that I knew who and what I was at the time and could have averted so much pain to the girls I dated as well as myself. This book was written to show you that the person that suffered the most was me. I don't want or need your sympathy. I am simply telling you what life had been like for me. I am laying bare my mistakes and shortcomings, knowing that some of you will judge me, some of you may feel for me, and others will be indifferent. All those responses are fine. I want you to understand that not all gay men want to deceive women. Don't get me wrong. Some men do. I can't speak for them. I can only speak for myself and my experience. I know pain very well. I've been both the recipient and the giver; neither one feels good.

I can't sit in judgment of men who live double lives. I don't know what they've gone through, nor do I know their circumstances. Are they living in secret? Do their partners know about it? I can't answer those questions, and neither can you. I can only say that I don't condone deception of any kind.

I also want you to know that some men choose to live in the closet because they aren't ready to be themselves. There may be repercussions from both a spiritual and socioeconomic standpoint. There may be issues regarding family that they aren't ready to deal with. I've experienced it. I've been passed up for promotions at previous places of employment and experienced blatant discrimination because of who I was. I've been branded a liar by my constituents because I didn't own up to who I was when I knew that it wasn't emotionally safe for me to do so. The same people that branded me a liar will never know that the very reason why they felt that it was their right to brand me a liar is the same reason why it wasn't safe for me to be who I was.

As a gay man, you take a chance when you choose to let someone into your inner circle. I am very selective in that regard because I know that everyone that says that they are my friend isn't ... even if they are gay themselves.

I think that most men just want to live their lives in peace and be who they are without fear of retribution. I don't think we want to hear about who we are in church and at the same time hand over our hard-earned money, especially when there are important issues that need to be addressed to both heal our homes and families.

Even though there are companies out there that claim that they have zero tolerance for discriminatory practices based on sexual orientation, the viewpoints of individuals sometimes take precedence over company policy.

We have men that come out late in life. Families are decimated, and wives are crushed. Why this happens, I don't know. But families are not hurt any less if the father has left the mother for another woman than a man.

I don't have the answers. I only say that when I knew who I was, I had to tell the woman that I loved and hoped that she would understand. She did, but not at first. It took years. There is still something between us to this day, and we remain good friends. Whenever I see Trina, sometimes I am transported back to when we were a couple because she still has that way about her that made me fall in love with her in the first place. This is what makes her unique and special.

Not all gay men do plan to hurt you. Ultimately, what I've always wanted was to just be at peace in my heart and mind. I think there are a large percentage of gay men that share this particular sentiment. But despite that, some of us continue to struggle with who we are because what we were programmed to be as children may be in direct conflict with our true selves.

I've come a long way in owning who I am. The road wasn't easy. And even now as I write this, there is a small part of me that wishes that I were heterosexual. I know that I will never marry a woman, have children, and enjoy a life that I see portrayed in movies, television shows, and commercials.

I belong to a church where I can marry my partner, proudly call him my husband, and know in my heart of hearts that it is okay. But simply because we live in an age where the LGBTQ community have come into their own by way of having their civil rights acknowledged, it doesn't undo years of programming by society, church, and families.

SO WHAT NOW?

I believe that I lived my life for forty-five years in emotional darkness, more if you add on the additional years that it took for me to finish this book. I conformed myself to what I thought the men in my life wanted me to be, even if it was at my own expense. I've spent so much time believing the very worst of me or even what hateful people had to say about me. And if what they were saying happened to be true, I would blow it out of proportion and, for a short time, allow what they said to become my reality. It is always easier to believe the negative as opposed to the positive. This, of course, is contingent upon where you come from as well as what your support system was at various intervals in your life.

I've walked in darkness while searching for something, oftentimes not knowing what I was looking for. I realize now that if I had just taken the time to fall in love with myself as opposed to looking for someone else to do that for me, I would have been much better off. I understand now that what happened to me between the ages of six and fourteen wasn't my fault. How I responded emotionally, physically, and sexually to those circumstances is irrelevant.

My only regret is not knowing who I would have become if I had not been touched at all. I know now that the trajectory of my life had been changed at the age of six. Who I would have been or become will forever remain a mystery. And maybe it's good that I was changed because I never would have had the courage to write this book. At one point and time, I started not to. Maybe this is what God had intended for me after all. When I get to heaven, I will ask him.

I still live in the aftermath of what happened to me when I was younger. I still experience bouts of depression even though I am with my current partner. The good news is that those bouts of depression are far and few between. The hurt that I carry is still a part of me. It always will be. But you learn to deal with it, and then you move on. Every day is a new beginning, and with new beginnings come brand-new choices. I can choose to be happy or sad. I can choose to give my best or not. I can love as if this is the last love of my life or not. Ultimately, the decision is mine.

What I will not do is dwell too much on the past. I realize that I am more than the mistakes that I have made. I am more than my triumphs, disappointments, and shortcomings. This is not to say that I will never make a mistake again. I will because I am human. So are you.

You may be spending a great deal of time trying to figure out what went wrong with you or your life. You may be consumed with anger and regret. You may have difficulty trusting people, even those that have earned your trust. You may drink too much. You may do drugs too much. You may be consumed with one thing that may be unhealthy for you. You may. Many of us are and don't even realize it.

If you have ever wondered what was thrown out of whack for you, think back to any issues and/or circumstances that may have occurred in your life. One in six of us have experienced sex at the hands of a molester. One in six.

All you have to do is walk down a crowded street and count the men walking down the street. One in six men has had their innocence compromised. If you are gay and you have slept with an older man doesn't mean that you are okay, and that nothing has been taken from you. Maybe the circumstance was consensual. I assure you that if it happened before the age of eighteen, then it wasn't consensual, even if you think it was.

So what happens now? Honestly, this is up to you. I had to make my peace with what happened to me, and so do you. I had to understand what was taken and then work on correcting what was thrown out of whack for me. It took me over four decades to do so. It doesn't have to take you that long.

I am not a psychiatrist. I don't have all the answers. But I do have insight. I have insight to myself, and I am willing to share it with you. I told you my life story in the hopes that you would see similar patterns in your own.

You may have trust issues. You may have anger issues. You may have periods of sadness, or you may indulge too much in drink or any other recreational activity. You may have more issues than what I've addressed in this book, or you may have none at all. Not everyone that picks up this book will subscribe to the ideology within these pages. That's okay.

But if by chance, you do see a glimmer of yourself in these pages, maybe it's time to connect the dots and let go of some of the baggage that you've been carrying for much of your life. You can do it.

I know because I am still doing it.

I wish that I could tell you that it will be easy, or that you will only have to do it once, and you will be fine. Unfortunately, it doesn't work that way. Healing is a process that takes time. In many ways, healing is just like recovery. You have to work at it. Sometimes, it may mean forgiving the person who took your innocence from you. Many times, it means forgiving yourself for things that you've done. You may have to forgive over and over until it becomes a part of you ... and then when it does, you will have to forgive again.

For me, one of my turning points was learning that Stan had molested over fifteen boys in my school. I learned this by talking to at least two of the boys that had been his victims. One was in the same class as me, and the other was one grade behind me. That knowledge had changed what I felt about him. I thought that I was special. I thought that he looked at me as a special young man. What I realized now was that I was just another young dick. Sorry to be so blunt, but that's what it was. He didn't love me just like he didn't love any of the others. Once I realized this, it changed something in me. Why did the knowledge of Stan not really caring for me and not my uncle or homeroom teacher affect me so deeply? I don't know. Maybe it was because I thought that he really did. Maybe it was because of my age at the time, that these incidences of molestation occurred. With my uncle, I was six; with Stan, I was thirteen as was my homeroom teacher.

And what about Zeke who seems to the worst perpetrator of them all? He was the hardest person to write about because it was what he did that I erased from my memory over the years.

Would I have been gay if this didn't happen to me? Yes. I am convinced that I would have been since being gay is something that you are and not something that you do. Despite my previous relationships with girls, I still like men. I love men in fact. It just took me years to realize that no matter how bad I may have wanted to be heterosexual, it wasn't going to happen. I will not have a wife or sire children. With this knowledge comes the fact that I can be who I am and become comfortable in my own skin. There is no pretending. I can be myself, and if anyone likes me, great, and if they don't... well, that's okay too.

I've learned that life is too short to be unhappy. I can choose to live a lie or live in truth. I can choose to believe in a God that loves me or one that will forever condemn me. The choice is mine. People will not always like what I have to say, but at this juncture in my life, they don't have to. It doesn't mean that I don't have the right to say it.

We live in a highly judgmental society where many people need to feel better about themselves by making someone else feel as if they are undeserving. We don't have to subscribe to their ideologies. As men, half of the battle of life is just to survive and live to a ripe old age, and if we are fortunate, we may have found love, joy, and happiness along the way. I've learned and accepted willingly that there is more to me than what people may have thought in the past whether they knew me as the awkward teenage boy, the misguided young man in my early twenties, the battered addict that had been my existence when I was in my mid to late twenties, or the man that I ultimately became.

We all have points in our lives where we've made wrong choices or done things that we are not proud of. We have loved the wrong person or taken something from someone else that simply wasn't ours to take. We have lied and been lied to. We have lost people and have had others brought into our lives. Some of us have experienced the very worst in humanity, and others have given the best in what humanity has to offer. I have no idea where I fit in the grand scheme of things.

But this I know: I will continue to move forward and wash off what was done to me and try very hard not to let what was done affect those around me. I will make mistakes. I will be difficult and hardheaded, if not downright obstinate. But I will let the best of me show as much as I can. Reclaiming yourself isn't easy. In many ways, it's like working the twelve-step program that alcoholics work to maintain their sobriety. You have to work at it every day. You will not wake up and be magically healed. Life unfortunately just doesn't happen that way. At times, you will be angry, confused, or very sad. This is normal.

You may want to seek solace in the fact that no damage has occurred because of what was taken from you. I know because I've been there. But honestly, sometimes I just want to walk into the light and bask in the warming rays of the sun and believe that I am awesome with all my faults and shortcomings. And maybe that is the way it's supposed to be. There's a saying that the drag queen RuPaul says that I think about from time to time. The saying is, "If you don't love yourself, how the hell can you love somebody else?"

I believe that. Before you fall in love with someone, you first have to fall in love with yourself. Along the way, if you choose to believe, fall in love with God. It is my belief that God is love in its purest form. It's man that hates, and it is also man that corrupts. We don't have to listen to what man says. We can believe in ourselves and try our damnest to live good wholesome lives. We can set aside our destructive behaviors and replace them with new ones. The choice is ours. By saying this, I am not by any means trying to minimize your battles. I don't know your struggles just like I don't know your strengths. I do know that you have both. We all have something that we struggle with, and we all have something inherently good in us.

I can tell you that you will not reclaim the person that you would have been if you had never been touched. But you can make yourself into a better person. You can make yourself into the image that you want and need to be. The choice is yours.

WEBSITES AND LINKS

Websites for assistance for survivors are listed below:

1 in 6 Website
https://1in6.org/family-and-friends/myths/

Helpguide.org
http://www.helpguide.org/articles/abuse/child-abuse-and-neglect.htm

The Men's Project
http://www.themensproject.ca/TenFactsAboutSexualAbuseOfBoys

TeenHelp.com
http://www.teenhelp.com/teen-abuse/sexual-abuse-stats.html

Prevent Child Abuse America
http://www.preventchildabuse.org/SiteAssets/docs/Sexual%20Abuse%20of%20Boys.pdf

Male Survivor
http://www.malesurvivor.org/myths.html

Single-Parent Homes
http://datacenter.kidscount.org/data/tables/107-children-in-single-parent-families-by#detailed/1/any/false/868,867,133,38,35/10,168,9,12,1,13,185/432,431

ABOUT THE AUTHOR

Being a survivor isn't what defines him. It is simply a part of him. In most of his darkest hours, he sought comfort in his dialogue with God and writing.

He has been writing professionally since 1989 and as a hobby for most of his adolescent and adult life. He's written for various publications, both hard copy and online. He's been labeled everything from being a hero to being blatantly false.

He's lived by the mantra that one event does not define you . . . It should only shape you.

As a writer, he does what he loves to do and adheres to the old saying, "Writers write."

MARION COUNTY PUBLIC
LIBRARY SYSTEM
321 Monroe Street
Fairmont, WV 26554
(304) 366-1210